CONCEPTS OF DHAMMA IN DHAMMAPADA

Bhikkhunī T.N. Tin Lien
M.A., M.Phil

EASTERN BOOK LINKERS
DELHI : : (INDIA)

Publishers :
EASTERN BOOK LINKERS
5825, New Chandrawal, Jawahar Nagar,
Delhi-110007 Ph.: 2520287

First Edition : 1996

ISBN : 81-86339-40-X

Laser typesetting & Printing at :
UNIQUE PRINT MEDIA
Phone : 7252362

DEDICATED
TO
MY UPAJJHĀYINĪ
THERĪ T.N. HUYNH LIEN,
WHO PUT ME ON THE BUDDHA-TRUTH.

PREFACE

"Dhamma" is a technical term which seems familiar, in fact, so much complicated in philosophical field. It is held on the tongue of philosophers when discussing about the world and the view of life. Especially Buddhist people get used to the term Dhamma throuth Tipiṭaka, the sacred scriptures containing what the Buddha taught during the course of his life.

The Dhammapada is the most popular and best-known text of the pāli Suttapitaka. It is a collection of chosen verses picked up from various discourses of five Nikāyas. It is pregnant with great significance of practical moral and essential philosophy of Buddhism. Carefully studying concepts of Dhamma in the Dhammapada also help in catching the most specific concepts of the term Dhamma in the entire system of doctrine of the Buddha.

Besides its familiar meanings such as Dhamma as Religion, Duty, or Law which are mentioned in Vedic and Puranic texts and literatures, the concepts of Dhamma in Buddhism are something attractive which ceaselessly urge many researchers to study it under various fields.

In the Dhammapada, the term Dhamma appeared in 48 verses which are summarized in following nine concepts. Just in the first and second verses, Dhamma is used in the sense of cetasikas (mental states). It is also used as law in verse 5; or as Buddhavacana (Buddha's teachings) in various verses. Dhamma also as means, way, state, practice and nature. In some other cases, Dhamma refered to phenomena, Budhipakkhiya Dhammā (Factors of Enlightenment) or as Samatha and Vipassanā; or as Nine Transcendentals and also as the Truth. Each concept is comprehensively discussed in each section of the present book.

In a nutshell, the term Dhamma in the Dhammapada comprises almost the entire teaching of the Buddha in Tipiṭaka. Readers are expected not only to read for getting knowledge but also for practising it in daily life. This is the only way we can get more benefit which can be regarded as the true value of Buddha's teaching.

Being earnestly encouraged by my supervisor, Dr. Bhikkhu Satyapala, Reader in Buddhist Studies, D.U., as well as the great approval of my good friends, who have gone through this work, I boldly let it published to contribute a tender part in the research field of Buddhism.

Sincerely received all good advices from my superiors and readers.

Delhi, INDIA
08-6-1995

Bhikkhunī T.N. TIN LIEN
NGOC PHUONG VIHĀRA
498/1, LE QUANG DINH, GOVAP,
HO CHI MINH CITY-VIETNAM

CONTENTS

LIST OF ABBREVIATIONS.

A.	:	Anguttara Nikāya.
Com.	:	Commentary.
D.	:	Dīgha Nikāya.
Dhp.	:	Dhammapada.
fn.	:	Footnotes.
J.	:	Jātaka.
M.	:	Majjhima Nikāya.
P.E.Dict.	:	Pāli English Dictionary
S.	:	Saṁyutta Nikāya.
Skt.	:	Sanskrit.
V.	:	Verse.
Vin.	:	Vinaya Piṭaka.

CHAPTER I

INTRODUCTION

The Buddha due to a great cause appeared in this world. It is to show human-beings their ultimate wisdom, how to use it and how to live with it. It is to show the only Holy Path through which men can destroy their sufferings forever, cut off the circle of birth and death forever and get ultimate peace forever. All the Buddha's teachings during the course of 45 years of his life sealed in Sangha's heart, is called Buddhavacana.

Buddhavacana (Buddha + Vacana) means the Teachings of the Buddha. Its technical word is *Piṭaka* which has been used in the sense of:

- *Pariyatti,*
- *Paṭipatti* and
- *Bhājana.*

Pariyatti[1] means the scriptures themselves as a body which is handed down through oral tradition.

Paṭipatti[2] from paṭi+pad, "the way", method, practice, performance....And *Bhājana*[3] means a bowl, vessel, dish, generally a container.

When mentioning the term *"Piṭaka"* we at once direct the mind to the third meaning. Originally, it means "basket". This term appears in many *Suttas* as

---

1. T.W. Rhys Davids and William, The Pali Text Society's Pali English Dictionary, London, The Pali Text Society, 1972, p.432.
2. Ibid: 396
3. Ibid:501

a compound word along with the term *"Kuddāla"* (a spade or a hoe) such as in Vin.III 47; D.I. 101; M.I. 127; S.II 88; S.V. 53; A.I. 204; A.II 199; J.I. 225, 336; *Kuddāla-piṭaka* "hoe and basket". From this explanation, the original meaning of the term *Piṭaka* becomes very clear. The purpose of this *"Piṭaka"* is to preserve and to carry earth or any such types of items from one place to another without losing anything. It is in this sense scholars have adopted this technical term to refer to a particular literature which preserves the words of the Buddha in its original form through oral tradition handed down to the student by their teachers sincerely. And a person when pondering and practising over these words even a sentence or a verse with a concentrated and faithful mind, he is able to uproot the weeds of ignorance and finally obtain the state of eternal peace that is called *Nirvāna*.

Among the ocean of *Dhamma,* the *Dhammapada* stands out as a diamond-island and glitters as a lighthouse which men cannot control the thirst of adoration.

Before coming to have the analytical study of the concepts of *Dhamma* in the *Dhammapada* Scripture, some necessary searches we should get through:

-Classification of *Buddhavacana,* and

-Introduction of *Dhammapada:* its place and importance.

CHAPTER II

CLASSIFICATION OF BUDDHAVACANA

The Buddha for 45 years preached the *Dhamma* in various styles of discourses, to various persons of various natures and under various conditions orally. After Buddha's *Parinibbāna*, a great Council (Ist) was held to collect the words of the Buddha from various sources, to recognize them as *Buddhavacana* and to compile them in a *systematic* order. In this process, the *Buddhavacana* was classified in seven ways as belows:

1. Rasavasena.
2. Dhammavinayavasena.
3. Piṭakavasena.
4. Kālavasena.
5. Nikāyavasena.
6. Angavasena and
7. Dhammakhandhavasena.

1. Rasavasena:

The water of all four great oceans obtains only one taste of saltiness. Similarly the entire *Dhamma* taught by the Buddha, although preached to various persons of various natures, possesses only one taste. That is the taste of salvation *(Vimuttirasa)*. *'Vimutti'* means freedom. Freedom from all evil forces, freedom from sufferings, and freedom from the circle of repeated births and deaths, that is Freedom from *'Saṃsāra'*.

2. Dhammavinayavasena:

The entire *Buddhavacana* in another way may be classified into two following divisions: *Dhamma* and *Vinaya*.

-*Dhamma,* the teachings taught by the Buddha for the benefit of all his disciples in particular and for all beings in generally called *Dhamma.*

-*Vinaya,* the special teachings which the Buddha taught only for his homeless disciples. These instructive rules help them in attaining the goal of their monastic lives directly, without any wastage of time and energy.

3. Piṭakavasena:

In another way, the *Buddhavacana* can be classified into three divisions. Each division is called *Piṭaka,* thus there are three *Piṭaka: Vinaya-Piṭaka, Sutta-piṭaka* and *Abhidhamma-piṭaka.*

3.1.: Vinayapiṭaka has got two component parts, *Vinaya* and *Piṭaka.* The term *Vinaya* has further been divided into 'Vi'+'naya'.

'Vi' means properly, correctly.

'Naya' means to lead.

Therefore that which leads one properly, correctly is *Vinaya. Vinaya-piṭaka* means the collection of the Buddha's teachings leading one rightly in the direction of threefold benefication namely physical, vocal and mental while he is living in monastic life.

"Because it shows precepts and principles, and governs both the body and the tongue, therefore men call this scripture *Vinaya*".[4] The *Vinayapiṭaka* consists of the following texts.

3.1.1. Sutta-vibhaṅga.
3.1.2. Khandhaka and
3.1.3. Parivāra.

---

4. Buddhaghosa's commentary on the Dhammasangaṇi, the Expositor (Aṭṭhasālinī), London, The Pali Text Society, 1976, p.24.

The *Sutta-vibhaṅga* is based on the *Pātimokkha*, a moral code of conducts of Buddhist monks, to be recited in the assembly of whole company of monks in every monastery on *Uposatha* days. It is the first part of *Vinaya* text and occupied with laying down and explaining all 227 rules of *Pātimokkha*. There are two kinds of *Vibhaṅga: Bhikkhu-vibhaṅga* and *Bhikkhuni-vibhaṅga*.

Khandhaka represents the positive counterpart to the *Sutta- vibhaṅga*. They contain the regulations leading the monkhood life in the monastic Order like ordination ceremony, monsoon restrict, dress, shoes, etc. including the record of life of the Buddha from the time of his Enlightenment upto the formation of the first *Vihāra*, and the accounts of the first two councils.

Parivāra is the last book of the *Vinaya piṭaka* and it is the sort of resume of the preceding texts.

3.2. Suttapiṭaka is the second collection of the teachings of the Buddha. The word *Sutta* has got two component parts: 'Su'+'utta'.

'Su' means well.

'Utta' means preaching (discourse).

Therefore it is the collection of the words of the Buddha which has been preached well and nicely.

Buddhaghosa explained the meaning of *Suttapiṭaka* as follows.

"This scripture shows, expresses, fructifies, yields, guards the good and is unto the wise; a plumb-line; therefore sutta is its name."

(For it shows what is good for the good of self and others. It is well expressed to suit the wishes of the audience. It has been said that it fructifies the good, as crops fructify their fruit, that it yields the good as a cow yields milk; and that it well protects and guards the good. It is a measure to the wise as the plumbline is to carpenters. And just as flowers strung together are not scattered nor destroyed so the good strung together by it does not perish).

Suttapiṭaka is divided into five *collections* or *Nikāyas (Āgamas)*. They are.

3.2.1. Dīghanikāya.
3.2.2. Majjhimanikāya.
3.2.3. Saṁyuttanikāya.
3.2.4. Anguttaranikāya and,
3.2.5. Khuddakanikāya.

Dīghanikāya is the first *Nikāya* of the *Sutta- piṭaka* and is a collection of long discourses consisting of 34 *Suttas* beginning with *Brahmajālasutta*. It is divided into three parts *(vagga)* namely:

Sīlakkhandhavagga	:	13 Suttas.
Mahāvagga	:	11 Suttas and
Pāṭikavagga	:	10 Suttas.

The second *Nikāya* of the *Suttapiṭaka* is *Majjhimanikāya,* being known as the middle collection or the collection of the discourses of medium length, consisting of 152 *Suttas,* begining with the *Mūlapariyāya sutta,* and it is divided into three groups called *paṇṇāsa* namely:

Mūlapaṇṇāsa	:	50 *Suttas*.
Majjhimapaṇṇāsa	:	50 *Suttas* and,
Uparipaṇṇāsa	:	52 *Suttas*.

Saṁyuttanikāya is the collection of joined or connected Suttas consisting of 56 groups with 7762 *Suttas* beginning with the *Oghataraṇasutta.*

Anguttaranikāya is the fourth *Nikāya* of the *Suttapiṭaka,* collection of *Dhammas* characterised by numerical groupings and arranged serially in an ascending order. It consists of 9557 *Suttas* beginning with *Cittapariyādāna* and is divided into 11 *Nipātas.*

Khuddakanikāya is the last *Nikāya* of the *Suttapiṭaka*, collecting of the small *suttas* and divided into fifteen texts.

3.3. The third collection of the teachings of the Buddha is called **Abhidhammapiṭaka.** Here the word *Abhidhamma* has got two component *parts:* Abhi+Dhamma.

'Abhi' is a prefix which means excellent, profound.

'Dhamma' here refers to the four reals of *Abhidhamma* Philosophy namely *Citta, Cetasika, Rūpa* and *Nibbāna.* Since is deals with the ultimate truth and the philosophical principles it is called a special type of teaching.

Various meanings of the word *"Abhi"* were showed by Budhaghosa in his definition of *Abhidhamma* in the *Aṭṭhasālinī:*

"Because this book shows things that suffer growth, of proper attributes, to be revered, well differentiated, and of worth surpassing, Abhidhamma is its name." *Abhidhamma* consists of seven books:

3.3.1. The *Dhammasaṅgaṇi* deals with psychological phenomena.

3.3.2. The *Vibhaṅga,* "differentiation", a suppliment and continuation of the preceding books.

3.3.3. The *Dhātukathā,* "discussion of the elements," deals with psychic phenomena and their relation to the categories.

3.3.4. The *Puggalapaññatti,* "description of individuals", deals with the various personalities and the character in the form of questions and answers.

3.3.5. The *Kathāvatthu,* it is perhaps historically the most important book in the *Abhidhamma.* It deals with metaphysical questions.

3.3.6. The *Yamaka,* book of pairs on applied logic.

3.3.7. The *Paṭṭhānappakaraṇa* or *Mahāpaṭṭhāna* is a voluminous work on causality.

Threefold basket is collectively known under the name *Tipiṭaka* (Skt. *Tripiṭaka*).

A chart will make it clear as belows.

TIPITAKA

ABHIDHAMMAPIṬAKA

1. Dhammasaṅgaṇi
2. Vibhaṅga
3. Dhātukathā
4. Puggalapaññatti
5. Kathāvatthu
6. Yamaka and,
7. Paṭṭhāna

SUTTAPIṬAKA

1. Dīghanikāya
2. Majjahimanikāya
3. Saṁyuttanikāya
4. Anguttaranikāya
5. Khuddakanikāya

VINAYAPIṬAKA

1. Sutta-vibhaṅga

Bhikkhu-vibhaṅga
(Mahā-vibhaṅga)
Bhikkhunī-vibhaṅga

2. Khandhaka

Mahāvagga
Cullavagga

3. Parivāra

5. Khuddakanikāya

1. Khuddakapāṭha.
2. Dhammapada
3. Udāna
4. Itivuttaka
5. Suttanipāta
6. Vimānavatthu
7. Petavatthu
8. Theragāthā
9. Therigāthā
10. Jātaka
11. Niddesa
12. Paṭisambhidāmagga
13. Apadāna
14. Buddhavaṃsa and
15. Cariyāpiṭaka

It is the canon of the Theravāda school which itself belongs to the *Vibhajjavādins*, middle of the third century after the Buddha's demise. According to tradition, its compilation immediately carried on at the First Council of *Rājagaha* under the leadership of *Mahākassapa Thera*.

The Tipiṭaka along with its commentaries was fixed in writing only under king *Vaṭṭagāmaṇi Abhaya* (29-17-BC) in Sri Lankā., i.e. a few decades before the beginning of the Christian era.[5]

Pāli is the language in which Tipiṭaka is compiled.

4. Kālavasena:

This classification regards the time of utterance of the words of the Buddha. The entire *Buddhavacana* has been divided into three classes, namely:

4.1. Paṭhama Buddhavacana.

4.1. Majjhima Buddhavacana and,

4.1. Pacchima Buddhavacana.

Paṭhama Buddhavacana (*Paṭhama*=the first, foremost) is dealt with the words uttered by the Buddha immediately after attaining his supreme enlightenment under the *Bodhi* tree at *Buddhagaya*.

According to one tradition, Buddhaghosa, in the *Aṭṭhasālinī*, mentioning the following verses, is regarded as the *Paṭhama Buddhavacana:*

"Yadā have pātubhavanti dhammā ātāpino jhāyato brāhṃanassa, athassa kaṅkhā vapayanti sabbā yato pajānātisahetudhammaṃ,

Yadā have pātubhavanti dhammā ātāpino jhāyato brāhmaṇassa, athassa kaṇkhā vapayanti sabbā yato khayaṃ paccayānaṃ avedi,

Yadā have pātubhavanti dhammā ātāpino jhāyato brāhmaṇassa,

5. Dīpāvamsa XX.21; Mahāvamsa XXXIII. 100,101.

Vidhūpayaṃ tiṭṭhati Mārasenaṃ sūram va obhāsayamantalikkhaṃ ti (Vinaya I : 3-5-7)

[Lo! when appear true doctrines to the saint, zealous and thoughtful, all his doubts dissolve; He knows that all becoming is through cause.

Lo! When appear.......dissolve; He knows the demolition of all cause.

Lo! When appear.......dissolve; And he is as a light unto the world,

Having annihilated *Māra's* hosts,

even as the sun illuminates the sky,

Having dispelled the darkness of the night]

× × × × ×

However according to another tradition, the students of *Dhammapada* say that the following were the first words spoken by the Buddha:

"Anekayāti saṃsāram sandhāvissaṃ anibbisaṃ,

Gahakārakaṃ gavesanto dukkhā jāti punappunaṃ.

Gahakāraka diṭṭho'si puna gehaṃ na kāhasi.

Sabbā te phāsukā bhaggā gahakūṭaṃ visaṅkhataṃ.

Visaṅkhāragataṃ cittaṃ taṇhānaṃ khayamajjhagāti".

(Dhp.v. 153,154)

[Long I endure the circles of rebirth, seeking but finding not the architect, Rebirth continual is continual pain. But now have I espied the architect! Behold, you shall not build the house again.

Broken are thy beams, thy pinnacle destroyed. Now to *Nibbāna* has my mind attained. And now in me all craving is destroyed.]

Pacchima Buddhavacana-(pacchima: the latest, hindmost). Before entering the Mahāparinibbāna, the **Buddha** uttered the following last utterance:

"Handa dāni bhikkhave āmantayāmi vo, Vayadhammā saṅkhārā, appamādena sampādethā"

[Hearken now, bhikkhu, I tell you: conditioned things are subject to decay; work out your salvation with diligence!]

This is called *Pacchima Buddhavacana.*

Majjhima Buddhavacana-(majjhima means the middle). In between the before two periods, whatever discourse the Buddha has delivered is collectively called Majjhima Buddhavacana.

Altogether three periods they form Tipiṭaka.

5. Nikāyavasena:

The term *Nikāya* (Ni+Kāya) means the collection ("body"), assemblage, class, group.[6] The entire *Buddhavacana* has also been classified with regard to the sides, language, styles of the discourses. In this way of classification it has been classified into the following five *Nikāyas: Dīghanikāya, Majjhimanikāya, Saṁyuttanikāya, Anguttaranikāya and Khuddaka Nikāya.*

Here *Khuddakanikāya* refers to all the remaining words of the Buddha, excluding the four *Nikāyas*. That means the whole five works of *Vinaya,* the seven works of *Abhidhammapiṭaka* and the fifteen divisions of *Khuddakanikāya,* beginning with *Khuddakapāṭha, Dhammapada*....belong to the *Khuddakanikāya* in this classification.

6. Angavasena:

[Vedic *Anga* anc. Latin *"angulus"*= angle, corner, etc.... ungulus, finger-ring=Skt. *anguliya*.]. Literally it means a constituent part of the body. Figuratively it refers to a constituent part of a whole or system or collection.[7]

6. Pāli-English Dictionary, p 352
7. Ibid:6

Navangabuddhasāsana, "the ninefold teaching of the Buddha", i.e. the 9 divisions of the Buddhist scriptures according to their form or style namely: *Sutta, Geyya, Veyyākarana, Gāthā, Udāna, Itivuttaka, Jātaka, Abbhutadhamma and Vedalla.*[8]

Sutta:

The term *Sutta* (Su+utta) generally means well-explained, but here it stands for a particular literature consisting of all discourses bearing the name of *Sutta*, instructions, orders or rules-made by the Buddha.

Geyya:[9]

According to the *Aṭṭhasālinī*, all the chapters with verses in the *Saṁyutta-Nikāya* form *Geyya*.

Veyyākarana:

It refers to the entire *Abhidhammapiṭaka, Suttas* without verses and any other words of the Buddha not included in the eight parts is understood as *Veyyākaraṇa* or exposition.

We should make clear that *Geyya* means *Sutta* with verses and *Veyyākaraṇa* means *Sutta* without verses. So the latter is the same with *Sutta*. In point of fact,

---

8. Har Dayal metioned twelve in his book "The Bodhisattva doctrine in Buddhist Sanskrit literature" They are Sūtra (discourses), geyya (mixed verse and prose), vyākaraṇa (expository answers), gāthā (poems), adāna (solemn or trisumphant utterances), ityukta (quotations), avadāna (edifying stories), jātaka (birth- stories), vaipulya (extended treatises or longer texts), adbhuta- dharma (tabs of wonder, miraclass) and upadesa (treatises on esoteric ritual) (and vedalla, should be added). These twelve categories of scripture are collectively described as dharma- pravacana (exposition of the doctrine). An earlier list mentions only nine items and omits udāṇa, avadāna, and ityukta (p. 151)
9. Pāli English Dictionary, geyya p. 254; Veyyākaraṇa p.649; udāna p. 134; Navanga p. 348; Abbhutadhamma p.60; vedalla p.648.

Veyyākaraṇa is applied to those *Suttas* containing questions and answers.[10]

Gāthā :

It means verse. Here, it stands for the special class of *Buddhavacana* which are composed purely in verse-form, namely *Dhammapada, Theragāthā, Therīgāthā,* and pieces in the *Sutta-Nipāta.*

Udāna:

The special utterances which has been uttered by the Buddha while he has full of joy. There are 82 *Suttas* in this category.

Itivuttaka:

Means "Thus have been said". According to Buddhaghosa, 112 suttas taught in this way; "Thus was it said by the Blessed- One" etc. is understood as *Itivuttaka.*

Jātaka:

Composes of 550 birth-stories of the Buddha beginning with the *Apaṇṇaka.*

Abbhutadhamma:

It means "something wonderful, super-normal". Here, it stands for the class of *Buddhavacana* whereby the Buddha has mentioned certain special, excellent or marvellous qualities of some persons-*Bhikkhu, Bhikkhuni,* etc.....

Vedalla:

The term *Vedalla* is derived from the word *"Veda"* which means knowledge. The *Buddhavacana* which gives a helpful increasing knowledge and satisfaction to the learners is called *Vedalla.* It includes such *Suttas* as the *Cullavedalla, Mahāvedalla, Sammādiṭṭhi, Sakkapañhā, Mahāpannana, Saṅkhāruppatisuttaṃ.*[11]

---

10. The expositor (aṭṭhasālinī) p.33 fn2.

7. Dhammakhandhavasena:

Finally, from quite a mechanical point of view, the canon is divided into 84.000 *Dhammas,* i.e. individual pieces or lectures.

11. Majjhimanikaya I Sutta No 44,43; Dīghanikāya II Sutta No. 21; Majjhimanikāya III Sutta No. 9, No. 20.

CHAPTER III

DHAMMAPADA : ITS PLACE AND IMPORTANCE.

Dhammapada is the second work out of fifteen works of the *Khuddakanikāya* which belongs to the *Suttapiṭaka* in the *Tipiṭaka*.

It is one of the most best known works both in literary and ethical aspects. Running into verses with short and clear and convincing explanations, symbolizing with easily understandable similes, each verse of the book is pregnant with great significance which directly penetrates to heart of listeners. Reading *Dhammapada*, we have the feeling of confronting the Buddha himself, drinking the taste of his teachings directly from his lips, without interference of compilators. Besides, carefully studying the *Dhammapada* is essential for the correct understanding of the doctrine of the Buddha. Because of these characteristics, some scholars include this text in the list of classics of the world.

The word *Dhammapada* (Skt. *Dharmapada*) is composed of two components, *Dhamma* and *Pada*. The term *Dhamma*, Skt. *Dharma*, ordinarily translated as "religion" or "virtue", is used in very different senses in the different schools of religious traditions of Indian thought. To Indian mind, from the very dawn of Indian civilization, *Dharma* as the essential core which distinguishes men from beasts.

The word *Dharma* which may be compared to the earlier term, ṛta, and is derived from the root dhṛ, literally means "what supports or upholds". As the *Mahābharata* puts it. "The word *dharma* comes from "upholding" and human beings are held together by *Dharma*". It is "the final governing moral principle or ethical law of the universe". It is rooted ultimately in God. It is eternal and eternal is soul. For clearer, it is the basic principle underlying all our moral actions, the divine moral law, moral duty, the law of righteousness.

To Surendranath Dasgupta, in his "A History of Indian Philosophy" Vol. II (p.2-11) we have four stages in the development of the concept of *Dhamma* in Indian thought, i.e. *Dhamma* as the duty of following the Vedic injunctions, *Dhamma* as moral virtues of non-injury, truthfulness, self-control, etc. *Dhamma* as self-knowledge through *Yoga*. And finally, according to *Bhāgavatā*, *Dhamma* consists in the worship of God without any ulterior motive-a worship performed with a perfect sincerity of heart by men who are kindly disposed towards all, and who have freed themselves from all feelings of jealousy.

To Buddhism, K.N. Upadhyaya shows that S.N. Dasgupta has enumerated four different uses of it in the Buddhist scriptures such as:

1. Scriptural texts
2. Quality *(guṇa)*
3. Cause *(hetu)* and,
4. Unsubstantial and soulless *(nissatta nijjiva)* entity.

Jadunath Sinla had added one more to it is "the Law or Norm". Some scholars such as Mrs. M. Geiger and Prof. W.Geiger and Th. Stcherbatsky have tried to solve the uncertainty about the meaning of this term in their work *"Pāli Dhamma"* and *"The Central Conception of Buddhism and the meaning of the word "Dharma"* respectively.

To Rhys Davids in his *"Buddhist India"*. (p.292) etymologically it is identical with the Latin word *"for ma"*; and the way in which it came to be used in India in Asoka's time is *"good form"*. *Dhamma* has been rendered "Law" in his Pāli-English Dictionary (p.335) we may interpret *Dhamma* by the fourfold connection: doctrine, right or righteousness, condition and phenomenon.

The first meaning of *Pada* (P.E. Dict. p.408) is: (m) foot, (nt) step. Here it means a word (or a quarter of a verse), verse, *stanza*, line and sentence.

According to Nārada Thera, *Pada* implies section, portions, parts or way. So *Dhammapada* may be rendered, "Sections or portions of the *Dhamma*", "The way of the *Dhamma*".

Sāmaṇa "Wei-chi-lan" explained it in the preface of the *Fa-Kheu-King* that it is so called because all the verses, without exception are taken from some one or other of the accepted scriptures, and therefore they are called *Dhammapada*, Law verses (verses from the Law), because they are found in the canon.

Dhammapada is translated by Fausboll "collection of verses on religion"; B.M. Barua and S. Mitra approve of Beal's "Law- verses" translation; by Rockhill " The Law"; and by Max Muller "Footstep of religion", "the path of virtue" (or the Norm of virtue); by Childers "the footstep or footpath of virtue", i.e. the path that leads to virtue; while Spence Hardy still more freely called it "the paths of Religion"; by some others "the way of Truth", "The way of Righteousness".

The work *Dhammapada* is a collection of chosy verses taken from different texts of the *Tipiṭaka*, some traceable and some not. According to B.C. Law and also B.M. Barua and S. Mitra, Strictly we can speak only of four Indian recensions, viz, the *Pāli*, the *Prakrit*, the *mixed Sanskrit* and the *Sanskrit*. The fifth being added is the *Fa-Kheu-King*, a Chinese Recension in translation. Of these, the *Pāli Dhammapada* is the best known and most complete. It composes of 423 verses arranging into 26 chapters according to the subject related. The *Prakrit Dhammapada* is not complete. It is the only text of which a fragment has been preserved in *Kharosthi* manuscript, found among the ruins of the *Gośringa Vihāra*, 13 miles from *Khotan* in 1892. The Chinese *Fa-Kheu-King* original and the *Dhammapada* quoted in the *Mahāvastu* are regarded as ones in *mixed Sanskrit*. The original of the Chinese version of the *Dhammapada* incorporated in the *Chuh-Yau-King* and the *Udānavarga* some original portions of which have been found at *Turfan*, are works in *Sanskrit*.

[According to Samuel Beal in his preface to the Chinese version of *Dhammapada* translation, there are four principal copies of *Dhammapada* in Chinese namely:

1. Fa-Kheu-King.
2. Fa Kheu Pi-ii.
3. Chuh-Yau-King. and,
4. Fā-tsi-yāosin.

All of them refer their first arrangement to the Ven. Dharmatrāta (Ārya-Dharmatrāta). He was one of the great leaders of the *Vaishasikas* and lived about 70 B.C. and is said being the uncle of *Po-su-meh*, i.e., *Vasumitra*.

The original of *Fa-Kheu-King* was compiled by Dharmatrāta, brought to China by a *Shaman* Wei-chi-lan in 223 A.D. Samuel Beal supposed that Dharmatrāta while revising *Dhammapada*, added some additional stanzas to them, so the work became 26 chapters with 502 verses (it is not available now), and that this work was accepted by the fourth Council held under the presidency of his nephew *Vasumitra*, during the reign of *Kanishka*, and thus acquired the reputation of a canonical portion of the Tripiṭaka. When the work brought to China, Chinese editors (themselves Indians) when translating it into Chinese, added a number of stanzas in the different chapters. So the *Fa-Kheu-King* with Indian original book of 502 verses in 26 chapters is neither a faithful translation nor entirely a new compilation, but bears the character of both. It composes of 760 verses in 39 chapters.

The *"Fa Kheu pi-ii"*- i.e. parables connected with the *Dhammapada* was translated into Chinese by two Shamans-*Fa Kheu* and *Fa-Lih* of the western *Tsin* Dynasty (A.D. 265-313). It composes of 39 chapters identical with the *Fa-Kheu-King* but the verses (*gāthā*) are fewer. No agreement between the stories of this text and those given by Buddhaghosa.

The third Chinese version is called *"Chuh-Yau-King"*, i.e., the Sutra of the Dawn, or "birth of Light", consisting of seven volumes in twenty books, divided in thirty-three chapters. It is still refered to *Ārya Dharmatrāta* as its author. It was brought to China by *Shaman* Sañghbhadnga (about- 345 A.D.) and translated by Indian *Chu-Fo-nien* with the assistance of others (about 410 A.D.). As its title implies, it is a *Dhammapada* commentary rather than a *Dhammapada* text.

The fourth last Chinese version of a *Sanskrit Dhamapada,* known as the *Fā-tsi-yāo-sin. (Dharmasaṅgraha-mahārthagāthā),* compliled by Dharmatrāta, and translated by *Thien-si-tsāi* (A.D. 986-1001) of the later Sun dynasty (AD 960-1127). According to Dr. Nanjio, it is a compilation of the verses of the *Chuh-Yau King*.

× × × × ×

The *Udānavarga* is a pure classical *Sanskrit Dhammapada* text, translated into English by Rockhill who is inclined to identify the *Dhammapada* text in the third Chinese version *Chuh-Yau-King* with the *Udānavarga*. According to him, "the contents of the two works, as far as has been ascertained, are identical".[12] It also

12. B.M. Barua and S. Mitra (Prakrit Dhammapada) p.xv (Introduction).

contains 33 chapters, and more than 1000 verses, of which about one-fourth only can be traced in the *Pāli* text. The same collection is also found in the *Tanjur*, vol. 71 of the *Sūtras*, followed by a commentary, the *Udānavargavivarana* by the *Ācārya* Prajñāvarman, who lived in *Kasmir* in the 9th century A.D.

However, B.M. Barua and S.Mitra in their *Prakrit-Dhammapada* book show doubts about the authorization of Ārya Dharmatrāta to *Fa-Kheu-King* as well as to other *Dhammapada* works].

Pāli Dhammapada is composed of 423 verses divided into 26 chapters *(vagga)* as follows:

CHAPTER	TITLE OF CHAPTER		No. of Verses	No. of Stories
I	Yamakavagga	(Pairs)	20	14
II	Appamādvagga	(Mindfulness)	12	9
III	Cittavagga	(Mind)	11	9
IV	Pupphavagga	(Flowers)	16	12
V	Bālavagga	(Fool)	16	15
VI	Paṇḍitavagga	(Wise)	14	11
VII	Arahantavagga	(Arahat)	10	10
VIII	Sahassavagga	(Thousand)	16	14
IX	Pāpavagga	(Evil)	13	12
X	Daṇḍavagga	(Punishment)	17	11
XI	Jarāvagga	(Ageing)	11	9
XII	Attavagga	(Self)	10	10
XIII	Lokavagga	(World)	12	11
XIV	Buddhavagga	(Buddha)	18	9
XV	Sukhavagga	(Happiness)	12	8
XVI	Piyavagga	(Affection)	12	9
XVII	Kodhavagga	(Anger)	14	8
XVIII	Malavagga	(Impurities)	21	21
XIX	Dhammaṭṭhavagga	(Just or Righteous)	17	10
XX	Maggavagga	(Path)	17	12

XXI	Pakiṇṇakavagga (Miscellaneous)	16	9
XXII	Nirayavagga(Chapter on Niraya)	14	9
XXIII	Nāgavagga (Elephant)	14	8
XXIV	Taṇhāvagga (Craving)	26	12
XXV	Bhikkhuvagga (Bhikkhu)	23	12
XXVI	(Brāhmaṇavagga)	41	40
	TOTAL	**423**	**305**

Regarding the time of collection, the date of *Dhammapada* must depend on the date of the *Tipiṭaka* of which it forms a part. The *Mahāvaṃsa* (Chapter v, 68) confirms its existence of a few years earlier than the Third Council, the time of the Emperor's conversion to the Buddhist faith, for on that occasion, his teacher, *Nigrodha,* is said had explained to him the *Appamādavagga,* the second chapter of Pāli *Dhammapada.* It was, therefore, known in the middle or early part of third century B.C. To Nārada Thera and some others, *Pāli Dhammapada* might be orally compiled earlier at the First Council, it means immediately one month after the decease of the Master.

The *Dhammapada* is accompanied by the *Aṭṭhakathā,* in which details relating to the circumstances Buddha uttering the verses are given. There are 305 stories related to 423 verses. It is generally believed that the *Aṭṭhakathā* came into existence sometime in 4th and 5th centuries A.D., written by Buddhaghosa basing on Sinhala *Aṭṭhakathā* (Commentaries in Sinhalese) already in Ceylon. However, scholars after judging the style of writing, show doubts if Budhaghosa was its real author. How far these tales are genuine may be difficult to determine. Max Muller has already observed that such stories "may have been invented to suit the text of the *Dhammapada* rather than vice versa".[13]

13. Max Muller, Dhammapada (Introduction).

The *Dhammapada* has been translated in many languages of the world. It seems that every Buddhist country has its own *Dhammapada* translation with varying number of stories. The first edition was published in *Copenhagen* by V. Fausboll along with Latin translation in 1855. It also was the first printed edition of the Pāli text. But it is Max Muller, the first one to translate it (*Pāli recension*) into English in 1870. It was followed by A.L. Admunds (*Hyms of the Faith*) in 1902, by Wagismara and Saunders in 1920 and by F.L. Woodward in 1921 (*Buddha's Path of Virtue*), by Nārada Thera (The *Dhammapada*) in 1959; by Radhakrishnan in 1966 and by Thomas Byrom (*Dhammapada*) in 1976. The Chinese version of the *Dhammapada Fa-Kheu-pi-ii* was translated into English by Samuel Beal under title *"Texts from the Buddhist Canon known as Dhammapada"* in 1878.

CHAPTER IV

CONCEPTS OF DHAMMA IN THE DHAMMAPADA.

In the *Dhammapada*, the term *Dhamma* appeared in 48 verses and are summarily used in the nine concepts as showed belows:

Dhamma is used in the sense of:

-Mental states (Cetasikas)

-The Law.

-The Buddha's teachings (*Tipiṭaka*).

-Just, righteous means/way/state/practice.

-Things, phenomena.

-Path of virtue,i.e., *Bodhipakkhiya Dhamma*, 37 Factors of Enlightenment.

-*Dhamma* in "*Dvayesu Dhamma*"; The practice of Tranquillity *(Samatha)* and Insight meditation (*Vipassanā*

-*Dhamma* : nine Transcendentals-and,

-*Dhamma* means the Truth.

SECTION 1.

DHAMMA AS MENTAL STATES (CETASIKAS)

The first concept of *Dhamma* in the *Dhammapada* is Mental State. In the verses 1 and 2,*Dhamma* refers to this sense. A man is a composition of *Nāma* and Rūpa in which the former is formed with *Citta* and *Cetasikas.*

> *"Manopubbaṅgamā* ***dhammā***
> *Manoseṭṭhā, manomayā*
> *Manasā ce paduṭṭhena*
> *Bhāsati vā karoti vā*
> *Tato naṃ dukkhamanveti*
> *Cakkaṁ va vahato padaṁ,"* (Dhp. v.1)

[All mental phenomena have mind as their fore runner, they have mind as their chief, they are mind made. If one speaks or acts with an evil mind, suffering follows him just as the wheel follows the hoofprint of the ox that draws the cart.]

> *"Manopubbaṅgamā dhammā*
> *Manoseṭṭhā manomayā*
> *Manasā ce pasannena*
> *Bhāsati vā karoti vā*
> *Tato naṁ sukhamanveti*
> *Chāyāya anapāyinī"* (Dhp. v.2)

[All mental phenomena have mind as their fore-runner; they have mind as their chief; they are mind-made. If one speaks or acts with a pure mind, happiness follows him like a shadow that never leaves him.]

Mind is leader of men's actions and is performed by actions. Men are directly responsible for their actions. If one speaks or acts with a pure or evil mind, happiness or misery will follow him unavoidably.

Before coming to discuss about *Cetasikas,* it would be better of having a general look of *Citta.*

1.1.Citta.

The term *Citta* originated from the root *Cit,* to think. According to *Aṭṭhakathā, Citta* is the knowledge of the existence of objects. *"Ārammanacintetiti: cittaṁ" (Cinteti=Vijānāti).*

"Cinteti samapayuttadhammaṃ etenāti: Citta" that which mental states *(Cetasikas)* often relie on knowing objects is named *Citta.*

"Cintanamattaṃ : Cittaṃ"—Knowing is Citta.

"Citti karetīti : Cittaṁ"---that which makes beings' activities different is named *Citta.*

When being divided into two, *Citta* and *Cetasikas* are included into *Nāma,* while into five aggregates, *Viññṇa* is used. And the word *Citta* is always prefered when mentioning the different kinds of consciousness such as *Kāmāvacaracitta, Rūpāvacaracitta, Kusalacita, Akusalacitta,*

It is not fow people taking *Citta* (Consciousness) as a soul-a permanent unchangeable entity wanders from existence to existence, feeling results of *Kamma* like the wrong view of *Bhikkhu Sāti,* who declared in *Mahātaṇhāsaṅkhāyasuttaṃ* (M.Ixxx viii): *"According to my understanding of Buddha's teachings, this consciousness wanders and turns but has no change."* The Buddha scolded the erring *Bhikkhu* and reiterated monks that consciousness is due to conditions. Without conditions, there is no arising of consciousness. When six sense organs get contact with six worldly objects, there arise six consciousnesses: eye, ear, nose, tongue, body and mental-consciousness. Later, *Yogacāra* or *Vijñānavāda* school of *Mahāyāna* of *Asaṅga* and *Vasubandhu* added two more=*Manas* consciousness (the 7th consc.) and *Alayaviññāṇa* (the 8th consc.) So the total number is eight consciousnesses. It is known *Vijñānavāda* on account of the fact that it holds *Vijnaptimatra* (nothing but consciousness) to be the Ulimate reality. *Vasubandhu's Vijnaptimatra-siddhi* is the basic work of this system. It maintains that *Citta* (*Cittamatra* or *Viññāṇamatra)*is the only reality while the *Ālayavijñāna* contains the seeds of phenomena, both subjective and objective. Like the flow of water *Alayavijñāna* is a constantly changing stream of consciousness. With the realization of Buddhahood, its course stops at once.

Abhidhamma analyses *Citta* into 89 or 121[1]. If divided into *Bhūmi* (stage), it is of four kinds:

	(I)	(II)
-Kāmāvacara-citta:	54	54
-Rūpāvacara-citta:	15	15
-Arūpāvacara-citta	12	12
-Lokuttara-citta	8	40
Total	89	121

Kāmāvacara-citta (Kāma is desire and *avacara,* move) is a consciousness which moves in the world of desires. Eye loves beautiful forms, ear likes sweet sound, nose prefers nice smell, tongue wishes dellicious food, body likes smooth touch and mind attaches pleasant objects. Like a monkey remains on moving from one branch to another, similary, *Kāmāvacara* citta fickle, restless, unsteady and always roams in the world of desire.

Rūpāvacara-citta is the name of a consciousness which gets concentration on an object associated with one form and colour. This is *citta* got through meditation, exactly have to say *Rūpajjhāna*.

1. Bhikkhu J.Kashyap, Abhidhamma philosophy, Delhi, A.K.Distributors, 1982, Citta(P.1-43); Cetasika (p.44-86).

When the *Yogāvacara* practises *Arūpajjhāna* he will get **Arūpāvacara-citta,** a type of consciousness which develops concentration on an object having no form at all.

And **Lokuttara-citta** is consciousness of person who have gradually cut off one by one ten fetters *(Saṁyojana)* which steadily ties men in the circle of existences.

If analysing *Citta* according to moral, immoral, there are:

	(I)	(II)
-*Kusala-citta* (Moral consc.)	21	37
-*Akusala-citta* (Immoral consc.)	12	12
-*Vipāka-citta* (Resultant consc.)	36	52
-*Kiriya-citta* (Inoperative consc.)	20	20
Total	89	121

Moral consciousness, a consciousness is associated with moral states. *"Kusala-mūla-sampayuttaṃ cittaṃ kusalacittaṃ nāma"*. On the contrary it is immoral consciousness, *"Akusala-mūla sampayuttaṃ cittaṁ Akusalacittaṁ ñama"*.

Vipāka Citta (or Resultant consciousness) is the fruit of an active consciousness. The consciousness arises and sinks down. While sinking down it leaves impression on the surface of mind. Such impression is called *Vipāka Citta*. And, *Kiriyā Citta* or inoperative consciousness. It is the consciousness of an Arahat who has destroyed all worldly desires. Therefore his consciousness will not produce any *Vipāka* or resultance.

In the *Dhammapada* there is no verse related with *"Dhamma"* taken *Citta* as its conception.

1.2. Cetasikas:

The *Cetasikas* are such *Dhammas* which belong to consciousness. They constitute as the part and parcel of the consciousness. As the word *Sārisika* speaks of the *Dhammas* which belong to our body and the word

Mānasika speaks the sense which belongs to mind. Similarly the word *Cetasika* is the *Dhamma* which belongs to the consciousness. This can be understood with apt example.

Suppose we are coming to the university. On the way we hear the sentence that I am hungry, give me something. Hearing this, first of all each sound touches the ear. It means there arises *Phassa* or touch. Simultaneously there arises the ear-consciousness *(Sota-viññāṇa)* due to the coincidence of the two: sense-organ (ear) and worldly objects (sound). Following *Phassa* there comes *Vedanā*. It means there is the arising of feeling (agreeable, disagreeable or neutral). Again, the mind turns to know what type of sound it is. This is the arising of *Saññā* (perception, knowing). When it is understood that this is the sound of a poor man, there appears compassion towards him. It is the rise of *Karuṇā*. Then there appears whether helping him is good or bad. It is the rise of *Cetanā*. In the meanwhile, the consciousness is passing a process of 17 thought-moments to complete the course of cognition. After investigating the object with the assistance of psychic factors, then there appears the attitude of giving him something. Prior to this, *Phassa, Vedanā, Saññā, Karuṇā, Cetanā* are the psychic factors or *Cetasikas*. In this way *Cetasikas* are such *Dhammas* which constitute the consciousnesss. They are the factors of a consciousness. When there are *Cetasikas,* there is a consciousness or where there is a consciousness there are psychic factors. In this way, psychic factors are the part and parcel of the consciousness. They are 52 in number.

Generally divided, we can say there are three divisions namely:

-Aññasamāna Cetasika	:	13
-Akusala Cetasika	:	14 and,
-Sobhana Cestasika	:	25

The **Aññasamāna cetasikas** are psychic factors which are present in both moral and immoral types of consciousness. They are sub-divided into two:

Sabbacitta sādhāraṇa are 7. They are so named because they are present with all the 89 or 121 types of consciousness. *Vedanā, Saññā* and *Cetanā* (feeling, perception and volition respectively) belong to this group. The other four are: *Phassa* (Contact), *Ekaggatā* (one-pointedness), *jīvitindriya* (life-force) and *Manasikāra* (attention). Here we should give some notices about *Cetanā,* the most important *cetasika* in creating *Kamma.*

Cetanā is volition. It is the "motiveless inclination" of the subject towards the object when contact has taken place. According to *Aṭṭhasālinī* and *Vibhāvini Tikā, Cetanā* is that which co-ordinates the menal states associated with itself on the object of consciousness. "*Cetanā* acts on its concomitants, acts in getting the objects and acts on accomplishing the task,i.e., determines action.[2] Hence, when there is *Cetanā,* there is *Kamma.*

Pakiṇṇaka Cetasikas are 6.

Pakiṇṇaka means scattered. They are available with the consciousness in a scattered way. They are available with all the four *bhūmis* of consciousness but not all the consciousness of each *bhūmi*. They are: *Vitakka* (initial thought), *Vicāra* (discursive thought); *Adhimokkha* (staying without trembling), *Viriya* (Energy), *Pīti* (rapturous) and *Chanda* (strong desire).

Akusala cetasikas are the immoral psychic factors. They are 14 in number and available with all the 12 types of immoral consciousness.

They are : *Moha* (Ignorance); *Ahirikaṃ* (Absence of individual shame); *Anottappaṃ* (Absence of social sense), *Uddhaccaṃ* (Distraction of mind), *Lobha* (Greed), Diṭṭhi (False view), *Māna* (Conceit), *Dosa* (Ill will), *Issā*

2. Nārada Thera, A manual of Abhidhamma, Srilanka, the Colombo Apothecaries, 1980,p.86.

(jealousy), *Macchariyaṃ* (miserness), *Kukkuccam* (brooding over), *Thīnam* (Laziness of consciousness), *Middham* (Laziness of psychic factors) and *Vicikicchā* (Doubt).

Sobhana cetasika which means good types of psychic factors are available with all the *sobhana* types of consciousness. These psychic factors are 25 in number. They are sub-divided into four divisions namely:

(1) **Sobhanasādhāraṇā:** 19. They are available with all the *Sobhana* types of consciousness. They are : *Saddhā* (Faith), *Sati* (Mindfulness), *Hiri* (Individual shame), *Ottappaṃ* (Social shame), *Alobho* (Sacrifice), *Adosa* (Friendliness), *Tatramajjhattatā* (Balance), *Kāyapassaddhi* (Serenity in psychic factors), *Citta-passaddhi* (Serenity in Consciousness), *Kāya-Lahutā* and *Citta-Lahutā* (Lightness of psychic factor and of consciousness), *Kāyakammaññatā* and *Citta- kammaññatā* (Adaptability in psychic factors and in Concsiousness) *Kāya-pāguññatā* and *Citta-Pāguññatā* (Healthiness in the psychic factors and in the consciousness). *Kāya Ujjukatā* and *CittaUjjukatā* (Straight forwardness of the psychic factor and of the consciousness), *Kāya-mudutā* and *Cita-mudutā* (Mildness in psychic factors and in consciousness).

(2) **Viratiyo** : 3. Due to these psychic factors abstaining from Immoral Consciousness is possible. They are *sammāvācā* (Right speech), *Sammā kammanta* (Right action), and *Sammā- ājīva* (Right livelihood).

(3) **Appamaññā** : 2. They mean boundless, limitedless. They represent the psychic factors like *Karuṇā* (Compassion) and *Muditā*(Universal joy).

(4) **Paññindriya** : 1. It is the faculty of knowing, *Pañña*. It is due to this the knowing of different *Dhammas* is possible.

All 52 *Cetasikas* have mind *(Citta=viññāṇa)* as their forerunner, because, though they arise simultaneously with mind, they cannot arise if mind does not arise.

Questions might be arised such as from where these *Cittas* and *Cetasikas* are originated.

Practically we can say they are originated from *Bhavaṅga,* the stream of accumulated consciousness of past existences. The literal meaning of the word *Bhavaṅga* is the part of existence. *"Bhavassa aṅgaṃ iti Bhavaṅgaṃ."* A man has done moral and immoral deeds in his past lives. He accumulated the impressions or resultance of these actions. The resultance of these actions which is carried from the last state of existence to the present one flows on like a stream not remaining the same for two consecutive moments. This stream of consciousness is called *Bhavaṅga,* the sub-conscious activity of the mind in one life. This to a greater extent determines the life-process in the present state of existence. Here we should not regard this stream of consciousness as a visible stream like a stream of water. It is not like that. It has no real form. It is an energy.

Training the mind is the accumulation of good habits: using *Paññā-Cetasika* to prevent and weaken the arising of immoral mental states such as greed, hatred, ignorance, wrong- view, conceit..., to encourage and make habit the appearance of moral mental states such as universal love, compassion, kindness,sympathy, purefaith, energy, greedlessness...until our stream of consciousness contains all moral mental states and becomes pure and serene.

If we go further to doubt that from where the ultermost first *Cittas* and *Cetasikas* took root, the matter becomes too much subtle and complicated! We should await the answer from Abhidhammic scholars.

"The mind is very difficult to see, very delicate and subtle; it moves and lands wherever it pleases. The wise one should guard his mind, for a guarded mind brings happiness." (Dhp.v.36).

We've just had a general view of *Citta* and *Cetasika* and the relationship between them. Now coming back to verses 1 and 2, the word *Dhamma* here according to Commentary refers to three mental states, namely, feeling *(Vedanā)*, perception *(Saññā)* and volitional activities *(Sankhāra)*[3].

However, according to Nārada Thera, *Dhamma* in this case is used in the sense of *Kamma* or *Karma*, action accompanied with Volition (*Cetanā*). It gererally states all mental states (*Cetasikas*) in which *Cetanā* is the most important.[4]

So is there something unaccorded between these two explanations?

After the first sermon of turning the wheel of Dhamma, the Buddha preached the "Non-self" sermon in which man is simply composed of these five aggregates:

	Rūpakhandha	(Form aggregate).	RŪPA
CETASIKA	*Vedanā Khandha*	(Feeling-aggregate)	NĀMA
CETASIKA	*Saññākhandha*	(Perception-aggregate)	NĀMA
CETASIKA	*Sankhārakhandha*	(Volitional activities)	NĀMA
CITTA	*Viñāṇakhandha*	(Consciousness aggregate)	NĀMA

Analysing Phenomena according to *Abhidhamma*, there are four *Dhammas* covering conditioned and unconditioned things:

-Citta

-Cetasika

-Rūpa and,

-Nibbāna.

To Buddhaghosa, the term *Dhamma* refers to *Vedanā*, *saññā* and *Sankhāra*, but these three are 52 *Cetasikas*.

---

3. Daw Mya Tin, the Dhammapada, Delhi, Offest Printer, 1990, p.1, fn.1
4. Nārada Thera, Dhammapada, p.3, fn.2

(*Vedanā* is one, *Saññā* is another. The remaining fifty mental states are collectively called *Sankhāras* or volitional activities). Moral and immoral *Cetasikas* accompanied with *Cetanā* are performed by actions, beings creating *Kamma*. Due to Kamma-cause, Kamma-result follows, next comes *Saṃsāra*. Therefore, *Cetasikas* in which the most important is *Cetanā,* decide existences of human beings. That is the reason why Buddhaghosa here took *Vedanā, Saññā* and *Sankhāra* (=these three are 52 *Cetasikas*) as the meaning of *Dhamma;* while to Nārada Thera, the term refers to *Kamma* or *Cetanā* itself.

1.3. Dhamma as kamma (Cetanā)

An action *(Kamma)* will follow the rise of consciousness *(Citta)* and psychic factors *(Cetasikas).*

In *Majjhimanikāya,* the Buddha often confirms the existence of *Kamma* when saying that "with clairvoyant vision, purified and super normal, I perceived beings disappearing from one state of existence and re-appearing in another. I beheld the base and the noble, the beautiful and the ugly, the happy and the miserable, passing according to their deeds."

So the Buddha often warned his Bhikkhus and their disciples that : "*Kammā* are one's own, beings are heirs to *Kammā, Kammā* are matrix, *Kammā* are keen, *Kammā* are arbiters. One cannot escape from the result of his *Kamma.*"

There is no Buddha's other doctrine having raised so much controversy as *Kamma* theory. The Buddha declared no-soul, no-caste in one hand and in another impressed in rebirth along with one's result of *Kamma.* Is there something without harmony here? We will consider it in the course.

What is Kamma?

A *Kamma* (Skt.-*Karma*) literally means action or deed. In technical use, it means an action accompanied with volition *(Cetanā)*---intentional, conscious, deliberate, willful action---through body, speech and mind. An action without *Cetanā* is not named *kamma,* it is a mere action. In order to impress the major role of *Cetanā* in creating *Kamma,*the Buddha himself addressed: Oh bhikkhus; I declare that *Cetanā* is *Kamma.*

Every volitional action, except that of a Buddha or of an Arahat, is called *Kamma.* The Buddha and the Arahat do not accumulate fresh *Kamma* as they have destroyed all their passions.

There are two types of *Kamma* (in the sense of mere action).

-*Kusala Kamma* (moral actions)

-*Akusala Kamma* (immoral actions).

Kusala Kamma and *Akusala kamma* may produce their due effects with the interference of *Cetanā.*

We have four kinds of classification of *Kamma* (in the sense of volitional action).

(a) There are four kinds of *Kamma* according to the functions[5] they perform namely:

-**Janaka Kamma** (Reproductive kamma) -One accumulated good and bad *Kamma* during one's life which condition *Viññāṇakkhandha* and *Rūpakkhandha* of his next life.

-**Upatthambhakakamma** (Supportive Kamma), *Kamma* which exist or maintain the action of this Reproductive *Kamma.*

-**Upapilakakamma** (Counteractive Kamma) Kamma which weaken, interrupt the fruition of Reproductive Kamma.

-**Upaghātakakamma** (Destructive Kamma) According to the Law of *Kamma,* the potential energy of Reproductive Kamma could be suddenly stopped by a more powerful opposing *Kamma* of the past, just as a powerful

5. Bhikkhu J.Kashyap, op.cit., p.154

opposing force can check the path of the flying arrow and bring it down to the ground. Such an action is called "destructive Kamma".

(b) In another way there are four kinds of *Kamma* according to the strength of their effect, namely:

-Garukakamma means weighty or serious Kamma. This *Kamma,* which is either good or bad, produces results in this life or in the next for certain. If good, it is purely mental as in case of *jhānas* (absorptions). Otherwise it is verbal or bodily. The five kinds of bad weightly *Kamma* are:

- Matricide.
- Parricide.
- Breaking pure conduct of Bhikkhunī.
- Wounding a Buddha and,
- Creation of a schism in the Saṅgha.

This is also called *Ānantariyakamma* (unpreventable Kamma) because it definitely brings fruits in this life or in the next. If in case a *Yogāvacara* (who is training the mind with meditation) does a serious *Kamma* later, his meritorious *Kamma* and his life will certainly be affected. As *Devadatta* lost his supernatural powers and was born in the hell because of his plotting injury against the Buddha and creating a schism in the *Saṅgha*. As in case of king *Ajātasattu* who could not obtain *Sotāpattiphala* (Stream Entry fruit) due to the sin of killing his father *Bimbisāra*.

-Āsannakamma (a death-proximate Kamma)

This is the *Kamma* one does immediately before the dying moment. This *Kamma* is very important because it takes major part in the state of coming rebirth. As in the case of *Matthakuṇḍali* (Commentary of Dhp.v.2), a young brahmin of a very stingy father, he passed away with his heart in devotion to the Buddha, so he was born in the *Tāvatiṃsa* celestial world.

It is also in the case of *Pukkusāti*, a young monk who did not know the Buddha before, he met the Buddha one night in the house of a potter. After listening His preaching, he recognised the Buddha at the end of the discourse. With mind filled with joy he went out to search a begging bowl and a robe for an *Upasampadā* ordination, being gored to death by a mad cow, he was born in the realm of *Anāgāmi* stage (Never-return stage) because in the last minute of his life, he died with the mind full of joy of enlightenment.

It is also with *Mallikā*[6] chief queen of *Pasenadi*, king of *Kosala*. She led a righteous whole life. Nevertheless, it is said that the moment of her death she recollected her telling lie to husband, and as a result, was born in Hell *Avīci* for seven days.

Because of the importance of *Āsannakamma* some necessary ceremonies such as inviting monks coming to pray at the death moment of relative have been done. The purpose of this is to remind his/her good *Kamma* he or she has done during life and to lead the mind remembering the Buddha, Dhamma and Saṅgha.

-**Āciṇṇakamma** (Habitual Kamma). It is the *Kamma* that one habitually performs and recollects and for which one has a great liking. As in case of *Cunda*,[7] a pork-butcher for over fifty- five years. Before he died, he was in such great pain and agony that he was grunting and squealling and kept on moving about on his hands and knees like a pig for seven whole days.

-**Kaṭattākamma** (Cumulative Kamma) embraces all that cannot be included in the above three and actions have been immediately forgotten after doing.

(c) There are also four kinds of *Kamma* according to the time they take in giving their effect, namely:

---

6. Malalasekera, Dictionary of Pāli Proper Names, Vol.I p.154.
7. Dhammapada Commentary, Cundasūkarikavatthu, verse 15

-Diṭṭhiddhammavedanīya kamma (Immediately Effective Kamma) *kamma* which gives its effect in this very life.(1)

-Upapajjavedanīya kamma (Subsequently Effective Kamma)-*Kamma* which gives its effect in the next life.(2)

-Aparāpariyavedanīya kamma (Indefinitely Effective Kamma)-*Kamma* may produce their effects in any life in the course of one's wandering in *Saṁsāra*.(3)

-Ahosi kamma (Ineffective Kamma)-*Kamma* which is ineffective (4)

According to *Abhidhamma,* we do good or bad *Kamma* during *Javana- citta* lasting 7 *shana* (Ksaṇa) period. The result of the first *shana-citta* may be received in this life (1). The result of the last seventh *shana-citta* may be got in the next life (2). If results of these should have not been appeared, we name (4). The result of *Citta* between the first and seventh shana (i.e., 2-6) may be given anytime in course of *Saṃsāra,* that means its fruits may produce in this life or the next or futher (3). It is even Buddha himself and Arahats could not aviod from this *Kamma* as in case of *Cakkhaupālathera* who suffered blind although he was an *Arahat* (Dhp. com. v.1)

(d) The last classification with reference to the place where *Kamma* produce their effect also has four kinds namely:

-Immoral Kamma which produces its effects to the plane of misery of *kāmāvacara* (world of desire).

-Moral Kamma which produces its effect in the better world of *Kāmāvacara*.

-Moral Kamma which produces its effect in Rūpāvacara (world of the form).

-Moral Kamma which produces its effect in *Arūpāvacara* (world of the formless).

Now I think we are getting puzzled and tired with the jungle of *Kamma* and its complicated results. Men feel embrassed with their accumulated past existences and remote coming future. Jainsts hold the view of practising extreme austere to burn past *Kammas*, making moral *Kamma* in present which prevents the bad result of *Kamma* in future. The Buddha, instead choosing the extreme ascetic way, took the Middle Way.

"Not to do evil, to cultivate merit" to prevent bad *Kamma* in present and future. *"Purify one's mind"* to train mind, exchange immoral mental states to moral mental states till the extinction of defilements, attaining the liberation-goal.

But what is the motive to urge men creating past and present *kamma?*

-*Avijjā*(Ignorance) and *Taṇhā* (Craving).

Due to ignorance, men grasp the notion of self, my building, my car, my wife, my children, my fame, my position, my beauty, etc.,.. do not recognize all these "my" being temporary, impermanent, destroyable, men can do anything to protect these "my".

Due to "Craving" men tend to act depending on their own love or hatred, their mind cannot be judge and clear, not seeing objects with right view and right thought, from *Taṇhā* conditions *Upādāna* (grasping), therefore bad *kamma* is created.

Hindu Law of *Kamma* holds the view that *Kamma*, men create, produces twofold results. One affects the doer, another produces an impress upon his soul. Each act he does produces an impress upon his soul. When a man dies and when his soul escapes, the soul is full of such impressions. It is these impressions which determine his birth and statues in his future life. The Buddha maintained "No-soul", so where is the store of *Kamma*? What creates acts and what will receive the results of these acts?

In the course of cognition at five doors of senses *(Pañcadvāravīthi)* and the course of cognition at mind-door *(manodvāravīthi)* there is *Tadālambana* stage lasting two thought-moments *(shana)*. The function which is the recording the experiences of the object for memory. The merits, demerits, colours and shape etc. of the object is thoroughly preserved in the mind. So a certain writer on psycho-analysis says "*Kamma* is stored within the psyche (nerve-system)". We definitely do not regard *Citta* (consciousness) as identified with the nerve-system because of one simple reason is the material nerve-system being totally destroyed after death. In another side, consciousness is arisen due to conditions. Due to eyes and due to forms, there arises eye-consciousness *(Cakkhu- viññāṇa)* and so on. So then, where is *Kamma?*

"O Mahārāja", says the Ven. Nagasena, "Kamma is not said to be stored somewhere in this fleeting consciousness or in any other part of the body. But dependent on mind and matter it rests manifesting itself at opportune moment, just as mangoes are not said to be stored somewhere in the mango tree, but dependent on the mango tree they lie springing up in due season."

Just as wind or fire is not stored in any particular place, even so *Kamma* is not stored any where within or without this body. *Kamma* is an individual force, and is transmitted from one existence to another.[8]

Who is the doer of *Kamma?* who reaps the fruit of *Kamma?*

Says the Venerable *Buddhaghosa* in the *Visuddhimagga,*

"No doer is there who does the deed
Nor is there one who feels the fruit;
Constituent parts alone roll on..."

Volition or will *(Cetanā)* is itself the doer. Feeling *(Vedanā)* is itself the reaper of the fruits of *Kamma*. Apart from these mental states there is none to sow and none to reap.

---

8. Nārada Thera, A Manual of Buddhism, Singapore, Singapore, Buddhist Meditation Centre, 1990,p.81

SECTION 2

DHAMMA AS "LAW"

The second concept of *Dhamma* in the *Dhammapada* is the Law- *"a natural moral order"* instead of *"the divine moral law"* of Hinduism.

According to Buddhism there are five orders or processes *(Niyāmas)*[9] which operate in the physical and mental realms, namely:

-Utu niyāma

-Bija niyāma.

-Dhamma niyāma

-Citta niyāma and,

-Kamma niyāma

Dhamma in verses number 5, 24 and 144 take the meaning of *Kamma- niyāma* while that of verses number 256 and 257 embrace the concept of five *Niyāmas.*

2.1 Order of Act and Rerult (Kamma-niyāma)

'Order of Act and Result' means desirable and undersirable acts produced corresponding good and bad results.

In life, the law of act and result can be divided into two: one applies to communities or societies in which Law is made by legislature for the proper regulation and another for self- responsibility of men in this life and in the next.

The term *Dhamma* in verse 24 has taken the first meaning.

---

9. Ibid: 84

"Uṭṭhānavato satīmato
Sucikammassa nisammakārino.
Saññatassa ***dhammajīvino.***
Appamattassa yaso bhivaḍḍhati"

[If a person is energetic, mindful, pure in his thought, word and deed, and if he does everything with care and consideration, restrains his senses, earns his living according to the Law *(Dhamma)* and is not unheedful, then the fame and fortune of that mindful person steadily increase.]

The verse related to *Kumbhaghosaka,* a banker's son, whose parents was dead, leaving a treasure for him. Because he left home as a minor child, no one recognized him, he could not take it out to use openly, so he kept patient and laboured under the society- rules. Finally king *Bimbīsara* made him out of his secret.

The second meaning of the law of act and result is regarding men's moral self-responsibility. Act is the cause and result-its effect. Everything in the world is formed according to the process of act and result. As cloud is cause and rain is its result. As seed is cause and plant is its result. As love is cause, and grasping is its results. As hatred-cause and enemy-its result. So the Buddha has taught:

"Na hi verena verāni
sammantīdha kudācanaṃ
averena cas ammanti
esa ***dhammo*** *sanantano."* (Dhp. v.5)

[Hatred is, indeed, never appeased by hatred in this world. It is appeased only by loving kindness. This is an Ancient Law.]

The Buddha uttered the verse with reference to a certain women who was barren and her rival. Their past feuds as rival wives of a common husband; as a hen and a cat; as a leopardess and a doe; and finally a lady with her baby and an ogress. They were made to see that hatred could only cause more hatred, and that it could only cease through friendship, understanding and goodwill.

The Law of *Kamma* is as natural and necessary as others. As surely as water seeks its own level, so does kamma, given opportunity, produce its inevitable result-not in the form of reward or punishment but as an innate sequence.

When the time is ripe *"Not in the sky, nor in the middle of the ocean, nor in the cave of a mountain, nor anywhere else, is there a place, where one may escape from the consequences of an evil deed."* (Dhp. v. 127)

Arhant *Moggallāna*, the Buddha's most supernatural magical power disciple, have to suffer terrible death by gangsters due to the sin of killing parents in a remote past life.

Arhant *Cakkhupālatthera* suffers blind because in a certain past existence, he as a physician, out of anger made blind a trust-breaking woman.

Buddha himself and Arhants have to take barley instead of rice during the twelth year rainy season *(vassavāsa)* at *Verañjā* due to a past remote sin.

However it does not mean that all causes will bear fruit. We have examined *Kamma* with its classification. Among sixteen kinds of *Kamma*, there are four kinds with regard to the time they take in giving their effect, they are:

-Ditthadhammavedanīya-kamma: Kamma which gives its effect in this very life.

-Upapajjavedanīya-kamma: Kamma which gives its effect in the next life.

-Aparāpariyavedanīya-kamma: Kamma may produce their effects in any life.

-Ahosikamma: Kamma which is ineffective.

Why is there difference about the time *Kamma* giving fruit? Sometimes even no fruit? It is because there is minor cause or assistant besides major cause. As the rice-seed is the major cause to arise rice-plant. It is certain that there is no rice- plant without rice-seed. But the rice-plant which grows fast or slowly, or sometimes died under the earth depends on earth-qualities, fertilizer, water-supply, human's care, harming insects, weather and sunlight.

In the same way, two persons in the same time sowing a good or bad Kamma but their result of which differs. Why it is so? It's because between cause and effect, there are many elements affecting the progress of giving fruit. That depends on-

-The merits of the causer.

-The affect of **Āsannakamma** (a death-proximate Kamma)

-Objects Kamma related.

-*Citta* (consciousness) of the causer whether pure or not

-The psychology of the man who receives the result, and finally,

-It also depends on whether there is the appearance of *Upapilakakamma* (counteractive action) and *Upaghātakakamma* (Destructive action) or not.

-Firstly the fruit depends on **the merits of the causer.** Anguttara I chapter "Salt" told that just as a handful of salt was put into a bowl of water, the taste would be very salted. But if the same that handful of salt was put into a river, its effect is as nothing. In the same way, the same bad kamma was done but its result differs between the more meritorious person and the less one.

-**The affect of Āsannakamma (a death-proximate action).** Through the stories of *Pakkusati*, the weaver's daughter, *Mallikā,* chief queen of king *Pasenadi, Matthakuṇḍali-* a young brahmin of a very stingy father, we are recognised how important this *Kamma* is in deciding the coming realm of beings.

Majjhima-nikāya III, Mahākammavibhaṅgasuttaṃ No XXXVI, said: "The men, done ten bad *Kammas* were born into Deva realms, while anothers done ten good *Kammas* were suffered hell". That is because of the interference of *Āsannakamma* (men's death- time have wrong view or right view).

-Objects Kamma related.

The person committed killing parents, Arhants...., it means one of five heavy sins, has to suffer infinite punishment in *Avīci* hell. This sin is much more than killing an ordinary one. The sin of killing an ordinary one is much more than that of killing an animal. Killing a president of a country is pronounced death-penalty, while the highest sentence of killing a civilian is life-imprisonment.

About the different quantity of merits one got, in *Majjh.* I, *Dakkhiṇavibhaṅgasuttaṃ No. XLII,* the Buddha has taught: There are fourteen different kinds of donation according to the kinds of receiver. Giving alms to *Tathāgata-Sambuddha* is the highest from which one got unfathomable merits. Next is *Pacceka Buddha,* then comes *Arhanta, Arahattaphala, Arahattamagga, Anagāmiphala, Anāgāmimagga*....donation to keeping Sīla persons, to non-keeping Sīla ones, and finally to all kinds of bird, fish, animal generally.

-The result of Kamma depends on **Citta of the causer.** *Citta* is regarded as important in judgement to Buddhism. Depending on volition whether strong or light the result of *Kamma* differs.

"It is not just the quantity or quality of gifts but actually the manner of the giver. An affectionated heart is better than a good gift." The result of a charity *Kamma* is very much

depending on the donor's *Citta* whether pure and faithful or not. As example of the begger donating oil lamp to the Buddha, the light has continuously been brightened while hundreds of king's lamps were extinguished when oil exhorted.

We must have known the famous historical conversation between *Bodhidharma*-the 28th Indian patriarch-and *Liang wu-Ti*-Chinese Emperor in A.D. 526. The latter put the question that he built thousands of monasteries all over China country, so how about his merits? "There is no merit at all", there came the reply that was not satisfied the Emperor. *Bodhidharma* then settled in *Loyang* where he engaged in silent meditation for nine years, whence he received the title of *"wall-gazing Brahman"*

What is the reason as the Emperor had done such a worthy work and got no merit in return?

The patriarch stood on view of emptiness, mind has no attachment to any forms of *Prajñāpāramitā* to answer the emperor. Because the "real" charity is no charity at all. "Giving" without grasping will gain immeasurable merits. Because one who has any attachment will fall back to cherishing the idea of an ego entity, a personality, a being, or a separated individuality. Because having attachment that means there hold the idea of the donor and the receiver, there exists the distinction between "self" and "others'. Besides, if the fact that the Emperor built thousands of monasteries with the idea to satisfy himself with fame, it must be naturally less merit in return. The *Sutta* also said: *Saving all the mankind, it indeed is no one is saved that is Pāramita-conduct of Bodhisattvas.*

We have discussed the case of doing good actions.

In case due to the universal love for the majority, a Bodhisattva have to *"kill one cat to save hundred mice"*, kill one cruel person to save hundred others, it is sure that his sin cannot be counted equal to that of the robber's killing to rob a valuable property.

-The result of Kamma is also depending on the receiver's psychology.

There are three kinds of *Vedanā* or feelings: happy, unhappy and indifferent. To an enlightened one, with wisdom he knows the five aggregates being empty, he ignores with the arrival of any feeling. he always keeps his mind pure and joyful in meditating states under any situation: facing disease as well as healthy, in the jail as well as outside. The Buddha suffered pained when *Devadatta* pushed stone down on his feet and caused to bleed out, although physicall pain, his mind was kept calm and serene.

There is a Japanese story of a virtuous high-ranking bonze. One day, there is a *Seṭṭhi's* daughter illegally being pregnant in his village. Because of fright, she accused the bonze of the sin and when giving birth, the child was handed to him. The bonze kept calm to nurse the child under all the insults of villagers. Later, after years marriaged without child, the girl told the truth with her parents, then all of them went to the hermit to show repentance to him and asking to get back the child. The bonze serenely satisfied their desire!

-Finally the time to appear the result of Kamma also depends on **whether there is the existence of Upapilakakamma (counteractive action) and Upaghātaka-kamma (destructive action) or not.**

As in case of *Devadatta* due to past accumulated merits born in the royal relatives, enjoyed all kinds of worldly pleasures. When becoming monk, due to *Upatthambhakakamma* (supportive action) he attained supernormal powers which raised him a high-ranking disciple of the Buddha. Everyone gave much respect to him for some years. Because of the press of *Upapilakakamma,* he developed greedy in mind, requesting the Buddha to hand over the authority of the Saṅgha to him. So as a result, he lost his powers and was expelled from the Saṅgha. After all he did *Garukakamma* (serious action) which turned into destructive Kamma. He fell into hell in front of *Veluvana vihāra* although his duration of life was yet to finish.

Due to accumulated Kamma from existences to existences, beings go round in the circle of six spheres. *Janaka-kamma* (reproductive action) becomes habits, beings are sometimes urged resistlessly committing newly moral and immoral *Kamma* at the present which condition the future's ones. Therefore the Buddha said: *"one's eyes, ears, nose, tongue, body and mind are due to past Kamma. The actions of body, speech and mind in this life is new Kamma"* S.V, 1982 trans of Most Ven TMC, p.141)

All these past and present *Kammas* are due to our own making. There is neither independent soul inside the body to lead nor the desire of a supernatural power outside to force us. *"Kamma are one's own, beings are heirs to Kamma"*. So the Buddha taught *"We have to purify our mind"*, that is the departure point and basic step to enter liberation-door. That also is the only Path of *Sīla, Samādhi* and *Paññā* which every Buddha's disciples as well as Buddhist people must follow. That also is the reason why the Buddha praised Thera *Pilotikatissa*, when the latter did what should be done and avoided what should not and finally atteined *Arahattaphala*.

> *"Asso yathā bhadro kasāniviṭṭho*
> *ātāpino saṃvegino bhavātha.*
> *saddhāya sīlena cà vīriyena ca*
> *samādhinā* ***dhammavinicchavena ca***
> *sampannavijjācaraṇā patissatā*
> *jahissatha dukkhamidaṃ anappakaṃ."*

(Dhp. v. 144)

Dhammavinicchayena = (dhamma + vinicchaya) discernment of the Dhamma or law. It is explained by the commentary as *Karaṇākaraṇā jānanaṃ* i.e., knowing right and wrong causes of things.

So the verse is translated as follows:

"Like a good horse stirred at a touch of whip, be diligent and get alarmend by endless rounds of rebirths (i.e., saṃsāra). By faith, morality effort, concentration, and discernment of the Dhamma, be endowed with knowledge and practice of morality and with mindfulness leave this immeasurable Dukkha (of saṃsāra) behind."

Therefore we ourselves build our heaven, it also is ourselves who make the hell. We are the builder of our own happiness. It is we who make what people name "destiny". So heighten the sense of self-responsibility, to raise the role of man to the most important extent in the field of enlightenment, and to praise the human-world being the best among six spheres of *Saṃsāra* is a distinguished characteristic of the entire system of Buddha's doctrine. Without self-responsibility, the law of *Kamma* is not mentioned. Without self resposibility, the law of society is also not constructed because there is no base to execute. A society without law would be in great trouble when people's sense is not high enough, not strong enough to resist their bad instincts. *Laotzi* maintained that an ideal society is one without law. "The best type of ruler is the one whose very existence is unknown to the people. By his wise non-intervention he so influences them that they believe that it is by their own efforts that all results are being achieved". This can be achieved only when each one in the social community has a high sense of self- responsibility.

The Law of *Kamma* is very useful for men and society. Because it makes one be fear of wrong acts, encouraging one's good deeds, hightening the sense of self-responsibility, educating people to believe in themselves, in their own capability- capability of enlightenment, freedom from all defilements, they won't have the expecting help-attitude, relying passively or begging. No expect for help because there is no one else but ourselves.

"By oneself indeed is evil done and by oneself is one defiled; by oneself is evil not done and by oneself is one purified. Purity and impurity depend entirely on oneself; no one can purify another" (Dhp. v. 165).

The law of *Kamma* also open a hopeful sky for ones who are suffering bad results of past *Kamma.* Because there is no Kamma named *"fixed kamma". Kamma* can be changed or lightened if one's mind keeps practising the purification.

The Law of *Kamma* gives a clear explanation about the variation of beings: the noble and the poor, the beauty and the ugly, the lucky and the unlucky, the mystery of so-called fate and predestination.

Now the question could be raised: Why the Buddha obtained the existence of the Law of *Kamma,* in the same time He objected the Caste-system?

No caste is the special characteristic of the Saṅgha.

Just as all the rivers lost their separate name and separate existence in the ocean, it becomes one with the rest. *"Same is the case with the Saṅgha, when a Bhikkhu entered the Saṅgha he became one with the rest like the water of the ocean. He lost his caste. He lost his status: so said the Lord."*

While *Yasa bhikkhu* belonging to a noble family, *Aṅgulimāla* was a robber. While *Mahāpājapatī Gotamī,* a noble Sakya also a queen, Bhikkhunī *Addhakāsī,* a courtesan. And while *Nandā, Ānanda, Rahūla* belong to royal farmily, then Upāli, a shaver and Chanda, a chario teer-their servants. In order to show their willingness to lose their superior caste, the royal young group desired *Upāli* getting *Upāsampadā* ordination prior to their own.

Once the Saṅgha stayed at a place suffering drought. Everyone felt thirsty. At that time someone offered a little water. The problem arose among the Saṅgha: To whom the water should be served first? A certain Bhikkhu suggested that the superior caste deserved that favour. The Buddha felt very bad with that suggestion!

Why it is so?

-Because the Buddha with his supernormal eye he knows there are *Bodhisatta* incarnations due to their desire to practise *Pāramitās* to help people among society.

-Beings, accumulated past *Kamma* from long existences with the assistance of *Āsannakamma* (death-proximate kamma) make the performance of the Law of *Kamma* more complicated. One's life-time is only a twinkle in *Saṃsāra*-series of the infinite past behind and uncountable future a head. Beings are candidates of a long course examination. Should not bring marks and position to class five to settle for class six. Because there is the fact of one's own effort. He stood position 50th in class five but could get the first position in class six. Life is full of sufferings. Human's life is temporary and in permanent and infinitely burned in cravings, hatred, sickness, death, grief, lamentation. Why we do not give one anothers love instead of torture?

-Keeping superior caste in mind means thinking oneself higher than others. The technical term for this is *Māna* (conceit), one of the ten fetters *(Saṁyojana)* which will tie the monk with the permanent cob-web of worldly attachment. It must be cut off if the Liberation is his highest goal to achieve.

It's right time to drop the subject of *Kamma* and the Law of *Kamma*. Besides this process, four other *Niyāmas* should be considered.

2.2. Physical inorganic order (Utu-niyāma)

This is the seasonal phenomena of winds and rains, the unerring order of season, characteristic seasonal changes and events, etc.

Everything in the world seems freely existing and moving. In fact it is working in an orderly system named Law. It will not be let down in any script but it is the factual statement of what always happens in certain circumstances. That is the principle of life. Water from rivers and oceans is changed into vapour under heat. Vapour is accumulated to form clouds. Cold air makes clouds form rains. Rains form rivers and oceans. The circle keeps going on. The earth on which people live, hangs among the immense space. It turns around itself to form days and nights and moves harmoniously with eight planets around the Sun to form seasons and years. What will happen if it stucks for some times?

Mountains and forests and oceans on the earth also change in every *Kṣaṇa*. Secret law of life is formed lively there. The procedure of oil, coal, diamond, gold mines have vividly been formed day by day.

All these seeming unmoving and non-understandable are according to their own law-that is *Utu-niyāma*.

2.3. Physical organic order (Bīja-niyāma)

That means order of gems and seeds. Rice is produced from rice- seed; bean with various kinds being formed by its distinguished seed. A hen produces hen egg, not duck-egg, etc. If we have a look at man, we recognize that blood-O-children must inherit from blood-O-father. The inside bodily system is a wonderful machine! Every organ has its own function but interacting to each others.

2.4. Order of the norm (Dhamma-niyāma)

To Nārada Thera, the natural phenomena occur at the advent of a Bodhisattva in his last birth. To K.N. Upadhyaya, it is a Universal Law of righteousness.

2.5. Order of mind or psychic law (Citta-niyāma)

Citta-niyāma is an order of mind or psychic law. For example, actions of the consciousness *(Citta-kiccāni)*, processes of consciousness at five doors and at mind-door, arising and perishing of consciousness, constituents of consciousness, power of mind, etc. Telepathy, telesthesia, retrocogniton, premonition, clairvoyance, clairaudience, thought reading-all psychic phenomena which are inexplicable to modern science are included in this class.

Now we will discuss some aspects of this order of mind.

There are two kinds of objects *(Ālambana)*

-External objects: visible object *(Rūpa ālambana)*, audible object *(Sadda-ālambana)*, odourous object *(gandhālambana)*, flavour object *(rasālambana)* and tangible object *(photabba ālambana)*

-Internal objects: *Dhammālambana*, ideational objects. It composes of six kinds, namely: *Citta, Cetasikas, Sukhumarūpa, Paññattivasena, Pasāda* and *Nibbāna*.

Citta- 89 types or 121 types of consciousness.

Cetasikas 52 types of psychic factors.

Sukhumarūpa-subtle material qualities,

Pasāda-Sensitive parts of the organs.

Paññattivasena-terms and concepts and

Nibbāna.[10]

10. Bhikkhu J. Kashyap, Abhidhamma philosophy, p.110

Eye, ear, nose, tongue and body, these are called *Pañcadvāra* or the "five doors" through which we receive information about the outside world and the process of cognition that takes place through these is called *Pañcadvāravīthi* or the course of cognition at five doors. There is also a sixth door, called *Manodvāra* or the mind door. It is nerve-system through which we receive the internal objects. The process of this cognition is called *Manodvāravīthi* or "the course of cognition at mind door."

Of these two, the first (i.e., **pañcadvāravīthi**) may be roughly explained with a simile.[11]

A man, lost in deep sleep, is lying at the foot of a mango tree. A fruit drops down and rolls by his side. He is suddenly aroused from his slumber and strives to find out what was disturbed him. He sees the mango fruit nearby; picks it up; and smells and examine it. Having ascertained that it is quite ripe and good, he eats it. Here:

(1) The *"deep sleep"* is compared to the passive state of consciousness, flowing undisturbed by anything, either external or internal objects. This state of consciousness is called *Bhavaṅga*.

(2) *"Getting up and trying to find out what has disturbed him"* is like that hazy state of consciousness which is striving tø make out whether the stimulus external objects belonging to eye, or ear, or nose, or tongue or body. This state of consciousness is called *Pañcadvārāvajjana* (a state of awareness at five doors).

(3) *"Seeing the mango fruit"* is like the arising of the particular consciousness, either of the eye or of any other four doors of senses. This consciousness is completely pure and simple, free from any reflection over it. If consciousness of the eye is called *Cakkhu-*

11. Ibid: 1

viññāṇa, of the ear *(Sota- viññāṇa)*, of the nose *(Ghāna-viññāṇa)*, of the tongue *(Jivhā- viññāṇa)*. and of the body *(Kāya- viññāṇa)*.

Rūpa-ālambana	Cakhuviññāṇa	Cakkhudvāravīthi.
Sadda ālambana	Sotaviññāṇa	Sotadvāravīthi
Gandhā ālambana	Ghānaviññāṇa	Ghānadvāravīthi.
Rasa ālambana	Jivhāvīññāṇa	Jivhāravīthi
Photabba ālambana	Kāyaviññāṇa	Kāyadvāravīthi.
Dhamma ālambana	Manoviññāṇa	
		Manodvāravīthi.
		Pañcadvāravīthi

(4) *"Picking up the mango fruit"* is like the arising of a consciousness which marks that there is something existing in the world of reality. It only knows that there is something. It does not know what it is. This state of consciousness is called *Sampaṭicchana* (the marking consciousness).

(5) *"Smelling and examining the mango fruit"* is like the arising of consciousness which investigates and trying to understand it in the light of its previous experiences. This state of consiousness is called *Santīraṇa* (the investigating consciousness).

(6) *"Ascertaining that the mango is quite ripe and good"*, is like the arising of consciousness which determines the object to be as such and such. This act of consciousness is called *"Voṭṭhapana"* (the determining consciousness).

(7) *"Eating the mango"* is like the arising of consciousness which tends to adjust the object according to its own suitability. This is the most lovely state of consciousness of itself and determines its own attitude towards the object. If the object is agreeable, it is accepted and utilized. If the object is disagreeable it is rejected. The act performed through body, speech and mind resulted *Kamma*. So this act of consciousness is very important and is called *Javana-citta*. (the active consciousness).

After *Javana*, the consciousness functions as *Tadālambana* which is the recording of the experiences of the object. The merits, demerits, flavours, colours, shapes etc. of the object are thoroughly preserved for memory.

After functioning as the *Tadālambana*, the consciousness again sinks down and begins to flow as the *Bhavaṅga*, till it is disturbed by another objects.

Bhabaṅga is the under-current of our mind which is constantly exerting its influence upon our personality. It is the accumulated experiences of many past existences. It is the continuation of this flow, at the time of death, we get the *Cuti-citta* or the dying consciousness, on an object presenting itself as *Kamma*, *Kamma-nimitta* or *Gati-nimitta.*[12] The *cuti citta* arises and sinks down, which is the last phase of one's present life. Just after that, the *Paṭisandhi- citta* rises up in the next life.

Thus, this life being connected with the other, and the *Paṭisandhi-citta* having sunk down, the stream of consciousness flows on in *Bhavaṅga* state, like the current of a river, continuously, being interrupted at intervals only by the courses of cognition, till his death.

For clearly we can summarize the process of cognition at five doors as follows:

Bhavaṅga (1) — Bhavaṅgacalana (2) — Bhavaṅgaviccheda (3)

Pañcadvārāvajjana (4) — (Cakkhu)viññāṇa (5) — Sampaṭicchana (6)

Santīraṇa (7) — Voṭṭhapana (8) — Javana (9) — Tadālambana (10)

12. Ibid 162.
(1) Kamma : For example, killing in the case of a robber.
(2) Kammanimitta : an article that had been generally associated with the performance of that Kamma. For ex., sounds or cries of criminal.
(3) Gatinimitta: the sign of destiny that awaits him in this next life.

When the object appears in the range of senses, it creates a vibration in the smooth flow. The vibrated state of mind is technically known as *Bhavaṅgacalana*. After the arrival of a new object, this smooth flow of mind is disturbed. There is no flow at all. It is shaken and the mind turns to the new object. It is called *Bhavaṅgaviccheda*.

From state (1) to (8) each state takes one thought-moment *(Kṣaṇa)*. *Javana* state takes seven thought-moments and *Tadālambana*, two thought-moments. In this way there are altogether 17 thought-moments to complete the course of cognition at (Eye)-door [*cakkhu dvāravīthi]*.

The process of Cognition at mind door **(Manodvāravīthi)** can be summarized as follows:

Bhavaṅga	Bhavaṅgacalana	Bhavaṅgaviccheda
(1)	(2)	(3)
Manodvārāvajjana	Javana	Tadālambana
(4)	(5)	(6)

So this process is very simple. *Bhavaṅga, Bhavaṅgacalana,* and *Bhavaṅgaviccheda* are the three preliminary. They do not form the part of the vīthi, but they are essential for understanding it. The *Citta* or consciousness which forms in *Manodvāravīthi* are three in numbers namely : *Manodrārāvajjana, Javana* and *Tadālambana*. The *Manodvārāvajjana* takes one thought-moment, *Javana* seven and *Tadālambana* two. Thus there are ten thought-moments in *Manodvāravīthi*.

And there are altogether fourteen functions of consciousness **(Citta-kiccāni)** in one's life-time from the moment of entering into the womb of mother till he departs from this state of life. They are:

1. *Paṭisandhi* : Consciousness connecting one life with the other.
2. *Bhavaṅga* : the current of the passive mind.

3. *Āvajjana* : turning to impressions at the five doors or at the mind-door.

4. *Dassana* : seeing.

5. *Savana* : hearing.

6. *Ghāyana* : smelling.

7. *Sāyana* : tasting.

8. *Phusana* : touching.

9. *Sampaṭicchana* : receiving the impression.

10. *Santīrana* : investigating.

11. *Voṭṭhapana* : determining.

12. *Javana* : the activities of the subject.

13. *Tadālambana* : registering the experience.

14. *Cuti* : consciousness disconnecting the present life.

We have discussed about five orders of conditional phenomena. Here we can pick out verse 257 in which the term *Dhamma* is used in the sense of the Law.

> *"Asāhasena* ***dhammena***
> *Samena nayatī pare*
> ***dhammassa*** *gutto medhāvī*
> ***dhammaṭṭho*** *ti pavuccati"*. (Dhp. v. 257)

[The wise man who decides not arbitrarily, but in accordance with the law is one who safeguards *the law* he is called "one who abides by the law" *(dhammaṭṭho)*].

When deciding cases, one is often influenced by his own view *(Diṭṭhi)* or sentiments or fames or profits-generally, ignorance, so he is often partial in one side or another. If one weights the evidence intelligently and decides a case impartially, in accordance with the law, i.e., considering matter under the whole and as it is, then he is to be called "the Just" or "the Righteous" or "one who abides by the Law".

Here *"Dhamma"* adopted the general meaning of the whole five progresses of Law.

SECTION 3

DHAMMA AS BUDDHAVACANA-THE TIPIṬAKA

Dhamma in verses 20,38,60,64,82,102,182,190,194, 259,297,363,373 and 392 take the third concept of *Buddhavacana,* Buddha's teaching or the Tipiṭaka.

How lucky we are human-beings and having a chance to listen to the *Dhamma*! Although the Buddha passed away more than 2500 years, his teachings have been preserved in the *Tipiṭaka.*

Through *Tipiṭaka* what the Buddha taught?

3.1 *Tipiṭaka* summarized in Sīla, Samādhi and Paññā

To *Mahāpajāpatī Gotami,* who had asked the Buddha to give her a precept, hearing it she might dwell alone, solitary, ardent and resolved. "The Buddha replies," *Oh whatsoever teachings, Gotami, you can assure yourself thus: "These doctrines conduce to dispassion, not to passions; to detachment, not to bondage; to decrease of worldly gains, not to increase of them; to frugality, not to covetousness; to content, and not discontent; to solitude, no company; to energy, not sluggishness; to delight in good, not delight in evil": of such teachings you may with certaintly affirm. Gotami, "This is the Dhamma. This is the Vinaya. This is the Master's message."*[13]

The same question put by *Mālunkya's* son and the Buddha asked him "Cut of cravings and conceit".[14]

---

13. P.V. Bapat, 2500 years of Buddhism. New Delhi, Publication Division, 1964, p.388.
14. Anguttara-nikāya II, trans. p. 253.

But to *Punnathera* in the *Majjhimanikāya III, Punnovādasuttam No. cxlv,* the Buddha taught two things: *"Due to the contact of six sense organs with six pleasant worldly objects, if someone arises the pleasant, compliment, attachment, grasping in it, there is the arising of sufferings. On the contrary there is the cessation of sufferings."*

Through *Majjhimanikāya,* the Buddha often said *"One thing only does the Buddha teach, that is Suffering and the Cessation of suffering."*

To prepare some basic knowledge for Bhikkhus who were going to go to some foreign places to preach the doctrine, in the *Saṁyutta-nikāya III, Sāriputta* Thera briefly said: *"If someone asks what the Lord have taught, the answer is: My teacher have taught about the control of desire and greed to the five aggregates, i.e., form, feeling, perception, volitional activities and consciousness"*.

And to *Ānanda* Thera, who was in more than twenty years as the Buddha's shadow, answered to the same above question that *"what the Buddha taught is Sīla, Samādhi and Paññā."*[15] According to *Mahaparinibbana-sutta,* these three groups had, in fact, formed the substance of the farewell discourse delivered by the Buddha at the various places through which he passed in the course of his last Journey. And unitedly *Sīla, Samādhi* and *Paññā* was adopted by Buddhist people as the unique path by which beings definitely get free from misery of existences.

Sīla is "Buddhist morality", "virtue", which Buddha's disciples, Bhikkhu and Bhikkhunī, as well as Buddhist lay people voluntarily keep to lead the righteous way of life.

Samādhi, "concentration", is the fixing the mind on a single object. And, *Paññā,* generally rendered as wisdom, includes all the doctrines of Buddhism, that

15. Dighan:kāya I, 10

is to say, the Four Noble Truths *(Ariyasacca)*, the Eightfold Path *(Ariya Aṭṭhangikamagga)*, the Law of Dependent Origination *(Pratītya-samutpāda)*, The Law of Kamma, the Three characteristics *(Tilakkhaṇā)*, the concept of Five Aggregates *(Pañca-khandhas)*, mind-only *(Citta-mātrata)*, Concepts of *Bodhicitta*, *Brahmavihāra*, *Tathāgata* and *Trikāya*.

[*Sīla* will be carefully discussed in section 4, while *Samādhi* and *Paññā* in section 7 due to subject related.]

3.2. Buddhavacana, one of the Triple-Gem.

The whole *Sīla*, *Samādhi* and *Paññā* is collectively called the *Dhammaratana*, one of the Triple-Gem: The Buddha, the Dhamma and the Saṅgha.

"Buddhaṃ saranaṃ gacchāmi."
"Dhammaṃ saranaṃ gacchāmi."
"Saṅghaṃ saranaṃ gacchāmi."

[I take refuge in the Buddha. I take refuge in the Dhamma. I take refuge in the Saṅgha]

Dhammapada verse 296, 297 and 298;

"Suppabuddhaṃ pabujjhanti
Sadā gotamasāvakā
yesaṃ divā ca ratto ca
niccaṃ
buddhagatā/dhammagatā/saṅghagatā
sati."

Rockhill's translation quoted below: "They who day and night are reflecting on the Buddha/Dhamma/Saṅgha, and who go the Buddha/Dhamma/Saṅgha for refuges, these men have the profits of mankind."

It is said by B.M. Barua and S. Mitra in their *"Asoka's Dhamma"* that the conception of the Three Refuges *(Tisaraṇas)* in the *Dhammadāsa* (D. II p. 93) changed into the later poetical ideas of the Three Jewels *(Tirataṇas)* in the *Ratanasutta* *(Sutta Nipāta* and *Khuddakapāṭha)* in a century.

We take refuge in the Buddha because the Buddha was a self- enlightened One who found out the way of enlightenment and taught it to people. We take refuge in the *Dhamma* because Buddha's teachings or Sīla-*Samādhi-Paññā* is the only path as a raft with which beings are crossing *Saṃsāra*- ocean. We take refuge in the *Saṅgha* because *Saṅgha* is an assembly of persons who desire to lead an awaking life, who are practising, preaching and maintaining the teachings of the Buddha forever alive. It is by these reasons that Buddhist people willingly take refuge in the Triple-Gem.

3.3 Buddhavacana, a factual Truth.

This *Dhamma* is the Truth. It is the Doctrine of Reality. It is a means of deliverance, and deliverance itself...whether the Buddha arise or not the *Dhamma* still exists. However human beings due to delusion have not seen the *Dhamma*. The Buddha with his own struggle for the whole six years of practising severe ascetic one day sitting under Bodhi-tree, he engaged in meditation, finding out the Dhamma and became known as *"The Enlightened One"*.

"Whether the Tathāgata appears or not, O Bhikkhus, it remains a fact, an established principle, a natural law that all conditioned things are transient (Aniccā), sorrowful (Dukkha), and everything is soulless (Anattā). This fact the Tathāgata realizes, understands, and when he has realized and understood it, he announces, teaches, proclaims, establishes, discloses, analyses, and makes it clear, that all conditioned things are transient, sorrowful, and everything is soulless."[16]

This *Dhamma* is a Reality, everlasting, being the Truth. So before entering the *Nirvāṇa*, the Buddha taught *Dhamma* should be regarded as one's Teacher, as safe island, "Abide with oneself as an island, with oneself

16. Anguttara-nikāya I, part I, p.286

as a refuge, abide with the Dhamma as an island, with the Dhamma as a refuge. Seek not for external refuge."[17]

Sukho buddhānamuppādo
Sukhā ***saddhammadesanā***
Sukhā saṅghassa sāmaggī
Samaggānaṃ tapo sukho (dhp. v. 194)

[Happy is the arising of a Buddha. Happy is the exposition of the *Ariya Dhamma*. Happy is the harmony amongst the Saṅgha. Happy is the practice of those in harmony].

3.4 The characteristics of Buddhavacana:

The **Vinayapiṭaka** is known having been prescribed by the Buddha with three attributes, namely:

Ānādesanā : Order-preaching.

Yathāparādha-sāsanaṃ : According to fault, punishment.

Saṃvarāsaṃvarakathā : Restraint-not restraint discourse.

(1) Ānādesanā: It means the Buddha had prescribed it by pointing out these are not to be followed and those are not to be followed.

(2) Yathāparādha-sāsanaṃ: The Buddha gave the rules according to the wrong action. Rules was made gradually depending on case for the better.

In the beginning, there was no rule for the Saṅgha. When the organisation increased in number, rules were made as the occasion occured. For instance, the first *Pārājika* was promugated regarding to sexual intercourse, concerning *Sudinna*, the son of *Kalanda*. The second *Pārājika* was laid down regarding to the taking of that which had not been given, concerning *Dhaniya*, the potter's son and so on. The four Restrains *(Nissayas)* were laid down in the case of a certain *Brāhmaṇa* who

17. Parinibbāna sutta.

thought he should lead a religious life among the Bhikkhus to get advantages such as excellent meals and necessities for life.

The formation of monastic rules took place in the same way. Sometimes some necessary change was made for the better. For example, the first *Upasampadā* ordination is the so-called *"Ehi-Bhikkhu-upasampadā"*-the *Upasampadā* ordination by the formula *"Ehi-Bhikkhu"* (Come, oh Bhikkhu), said by the Blessed One. Later, the ordination by the "three *saranāgamanas*"- the person seeking the *Upasampadā* ordination have to repeat declaration of their taking refuge in the Buddha, the Dhamma and the Saṅgha three times. Later, some newly ordained Bhikkhu have done mistakes, rules were made for the candidate that he has to get for himself an *Upajjhāya* (preceptor) to instruct him to lead the righteous life in monastery. In case his *upajjhāya* was gone away or returned to the world, or died, the young Bhikkhus should choose an *Ācariya* and live ten years in dependence on him, and so on.

(3) Saṃvarāsaṃvarakathā : There are the descriptions of restraining and non restraining. We find a number of cases in which one is requested to put restraint, there are also cases of transgression.

Budhaghosa has explained **Abhidhamma** by giving three attributes, namely:

-*Paramattha-desanā:* Ultimate truth preaching.

-*Yathā-dhammasāsanaṃ:* as the things really are.

-*Nāmarūpa-paricchedakathā:* Mind-matter analysis discourses.

The *Abhidhamma piṭaka* is known as *Paramattha-desanā* because it contains teachings or *Desanā* which deals with the *Paramattha* or the four ultimate reals namely *Citta, Cetasika, Rūpa* and *Nibbāna*.

It is called *Yathā-dhammasāsanaṃ* because it speaks about the nature of *Dhamma* as it really is.

Again it is called *Nāmarūpa-pariccheda-kathā*, it means it is a discourse on the analysis of mind and matter. Here it can easily be said that mind first has been put into two divisions, *Citta* and *Cetasika*.

Now we come to the **Suttapiṭaka.**

The Buddha has preached *Suttas* well and nicely. He didnot start his teachings all of a sudden, but he took into consideration three important things, namely:

-*Ajjhāsaya* (intention, desire, wish).

-*Anusaya* (defilements, ignorance, hatred and *Abhimutti* (liberation).

It means he considers the right time when the listener is ready to obtain discourse; to the defilements of his mind, i.e., he has either more greed or hatred or delusion; and to the purpose of liberation.

So he gave the sermon with the help of similes, illustrations, parables suiting to the mind of person. For that Sutta is called *Vohāradesanā*. His preachings aim at to get rid of the wrong view of the people, so it is called *Diṭṭhi vinivethanakathā,* and the third attribute of the teaching of the Buddha is called *Yathānulomasāsanaṃ*. It is so called because it has been prescribed with the co-operation of the temperament and belief of people concerned.

The Buddha used to use simple and clear similies to suit each kind of persons. Such as to *Soṇa*, a skill in playing lute, he takes the example how to use the lute to convey the *Dhamma*. To the elephant-trainer, he talks about of training an elephant. When seeing a piece of wood floating about on the Gangā-river he shows it to compare with the lax attitude in practising *Dhamma* of some Bhikkhus.

Buddha's illustrations are easily understandable even to a child. As in *Dhammapada* verses 1 and 2, in order to show the fast connection between *kamma* and its results, the Buddha used the picture of wheels of a chariot following the hoof print of the ox that draws the cart and a shadow never leaving a person. To child *Rahūla,* the Buddha turned upside down the basin of water which *Rahūla* brought for his washing feet to teach him not to tell a lie in any case.

Buddha's teaching is suitable to the temperament and belief of person concerned. To *Bodhisattvas, Arahats, devas* he taught *HUA- YEN,* and *Lotus Sūtras;* to ordinary people he explained the Four Noble Truths, the Eightfold Path, the Law of *Kamma.* To people tend to attachment of beautiful forms, the suitable antidote is the practice of contemplation of the impermanence of *Pañcakhandhas,* of the impurity of the body, of watching the decay of a corpse. To person with much hatred, he should practise his mind with *Mettā,* loving-kindness to others. To a dullard like *Cūlapanthaka* he requested to keep in mind just a single word *"rajoharaṇaṃ"* which means "taking out impurity". To a girl going to marriage, to a king of a state, to a robber like *Aṅgulimala,* to *Nandā,* etc. the Buddha gave suitable advice and used different means to get them on the righteous way of liberation. And one who is taught by the Buddha or has a chance to listen to the teachings even a single word, if faithfully keeping in mind and diligently practising it, will get much advantage in his life. Why it is so? Because the Buddha's teaching has the characteristic of making the mind calm.

> *"Yo ca gāthā sataṃ bhāse*
> *anatthapadasaṁhitā*
> *ekaṃ* ***Dhammapadaṃ*** *seyyo*
> *yaṃ sutvā upasammati".* (Dhp. v. 102)

[Better than the recitation of a hundred verses that are senseless and unconnected with the realization of *Nibbāna,* is the recitation of a single word of the Teaching, if on hearing it one is calmed].

"Like a lake which is deep, clear and calm, the wise after listening to the Teaching become serene". (Dhp. v. 82)

The Buddha's preachings always aim at to get rid of the wrong view of the people. *"Just as, O Bhikkhus, the mighty ocean is of one flavour, the flavour of salt; even so, O Bhikkhus, this Dhamma is of one flavour, the flavour of Deliverance (vimutti)*[18] Buddha's Dhamma is likened rain-water. Depending on the kinds of plant-big, small ones or creeds-which the sum of water is taken. Similarly how much one gets advantage from *Dhamma* depending on the level of the listener's character.

To serve for that purpose, although there are voluminous volumes of *Suttas, Vinaya* and *Abhidhamma,* the Buddha shows only one goal: the sufferings and the cessation of sufferings. And the only way to get that goal is the Noble Eightfold path, exactly we should mention to be *Sīla-Samādhi* and *paññā.*

The way of *Sīla-Samādhi-Paññā* is trully performed through diligently and strenously bringing the Buddha's teachings in practice. *Dhamma* is just useful to someone when he deeply ponders over it, understands it and brings it into practice in every *Kṣaṇa* of life.

"Appampi ce samhita bhāsamāno
***Dhammassa** hoti anudhammacārī*
Rāgañ ca dosañ ca pahāya mohaṃ
Sammappajāno suvimuttacitto
Anupādiyāno idha vā huraṃ vā
Sa bhāgavā sāmaññassa hoti". (Dhp.v.20)

[Though he recites only a little of the Sacred Texts *(Tipiṭaka)* but practises according to the *Dhamma,* eradicating passion, ill will and ignorance, clearly comprehending the *Dhamma,* with his mind freed from moral defilements and no longer clinging to this world

18. Udāna. p.67

or to the next, he shares the benefits of the life of a Bhikkhu (i.e., *magga- phala*)].

"Though he recites much the sacred texts (Tipiṭaka), but is negligent and does not practise according to the Dhamma, like a cowherd who counts the cattle of others, he has no share in the benefits of the life of a Bhikkhu." (Dhp. v. 19)

The preacher who is well-learnt and preached the *Dhamma* but does not practise in accordance with the *Dhamma* is like a cowherd, who looks after the cows for wages, while the one who practises according to the *Dhamma* is like the owner who enjoys all the benefits being got from his cows. In the same way, the good pracher enjoys only fame and respect and worldly benefits from his pupils but not the benefits of *magga phala*, while the other Bhikkhu, though he knows little and recites only a little of the sacred texts, having a true faith in what he had learnt, devoted himself in pondering over it and practising it through meditation. Finally he eradicates all his defilements, greed-hatred-delusion, and attains all the fruits of Saints.

In another place the Buddha likened the well-practising *Dhamma* with a tongue which can enjoy the taste of soup, while a fool although living next to a wise all his life, his mind grasps in worldly pleasures, does not strive for Dhamma-knowledge, this fool just like "a ladle" which is in the big bowl of soup but cannot enjoy a single taste of the soup.

"Yāvajīvampi ce bālo
paṇḍitaṃ payirupāsati
na so ***dhammaṃ*** *vijānāti*
dabbī suparasaṃ yathā". (Dhp. v. 64)

[A fool even though he is associated with a wise man all his life, does not understand the *Dhamma*, just as a ladle does not know the taste of soup].

Therefore in order to make clear his own view of how one "versed in the *Dhamma*" the Buddha explained:

"Na tāvatā dhammadharo
yāvatā bahu bhāsati
yo ca appampi sutvāna
dhammaṃ kāyena passati
sa ve dhammadho hoti
yo dhammaṃ nappamajjati." (Dhp. v. 259)

[He is not "one versed in the *Dhamma*" *(Dhammadhara)* just because he talk much. He who hears only a little but comprehends the *Dhamma,* and is not unmindful is, indeed, "one versed in the Dhamma".]

Following this advice-paying more attention in practice than in theory-Buddha's disciple take meditation *(Dhyāna),* Calm and Insight, as the major means to get the Truth. This inclination gave rise the Ch'an of China and the Zen of Japan.

SECTION 4

DHAMMA AS JUST, RIGHTEOUS MEANS/WAY/STATE/PRACTICE/ NATURE.

Dhamma in verses 46,84,87,167,168,169,242 and 248 has got these meanings.

In verse 84, the term *Dhamma* is used in the sense of Just means. In opposite meaning is *Adhamma*, unjust, unfair means.

"Na attahetu na parassa hetu
na puttamiche na dhanaṃ na raṭṭhaṃ.
na iccheyya **adhammena** *samiddhimattano*
sa sīlavā paññavā **dhammiko** *siyā."*

[For his own sake or for the sake of others he does no evil; nor does he wish for sons and daughters or for wealth or for a kingdom by doing evil; nor does he wish for success by unfair means: such a one is indeed virtuous, wise and just.]

In verses 256 and 257 the word *dammaṭṭho* means "one who abides by the law" or in one word, "the Just" or "the righteous". And the Buddha have expressed how "Just" and "unjust"are.

"He is not just if he decides a case arbitrarily; the wise man should decide after considering both what is right and what is wrong."

"The wise man who decides not arbitrarily; but in accordance with the law is one who safeguards the law; he is called "one who abides by the law."

The term Dhamma is also accompained by some attributive adjectives such a *kaṇhaṃ, hīnaṃ, pāpakā*... to give a clear meaning of dark, evil way, evil state as opposite to pure, good one in verses 87, 167 and 242. They are altogether technically called *kusalakamma* and *akusalakamma*. (kamma here in the sense of mere action).

4. 1 Kusalakamma and Akuslakamma:

Akusalakamma is so-called because it is associated with the three *Akusala* roots namely Lobha, Dosa and Moha (Greed, Hatred and Delusion respectively).

On the contrary, there are three roots of good *kamma* namely *Alobha* (sacrifice), *Adosa* (friendliness) and *Amoha* (Right understanding). The actions associated with them is called *kusalakamma*.

"Kaṇhaṃ dhammaṃ vippahāya
sukkaṃ bhāvetha paṇḍito
okā anokamāgamma
viveke yattha dūramaṃ" (Dhp.v.87).

[The man of wisdom, leaving the home of craving and having Nibbāna as his goal, should give up dark, evil ways and cultivate pure, good ones....]

The dark states *(kaṇhaṃ Dhammaṃ)* are the ten kinds of evil deeds, and the bright states (sukkaṃ) are the ten kinds of good deeds caused by body, speech and mind. That is, the mind directed towards the ten kinds of evil[19] *(Akusala kamma)* namely.

PHYSICAL ACTIONS

1. Killing *(pāṇa)*
2. Stealing *(Adiṇṇādāna)*
3. Sexual misconduct *(kāmesu micchācāra)*

VOCAL ACTIONS

4. Lying *(musāvāda)*

19. Nārada Thera, A Manual of Buddhism, p.77-78

5. Slandering *(pisuṇavācā)*
6. Harsh speech *(pharusavācā)*
7. Vain talk *(samphappalāpa)*

MENTAL ACTIONS

8. Coveteousness *(abhijjhā)*
9. Ill-will *(vyāpādo)* and,
10. False belief *(micchādiṭṭhi)*.

On the opposite, there are ten kinds of meritorious deeds *(kusalakamma)* namely.

1. Generosity *(Dāna)*
2. Morality *(Sīla)*
3. Meditation *(Bhāvanā)*
4. Reverence *(Apacāyana)*
5. Service *(Veyyāccaca)*
6. Transference of merit *(Pattidāna)*
7. Rejoicing in others merit *(Pattānumodana)*
8. Hearing the doctrine *(Dhammasavaṇa)*
9. Expounding the doctrine (Dhammadesana) and,
10. Straightening one's right views.

We have known man is the owner of kamma, being kamma's heir. Therefore it is not only avoiding bad deeds but good deeds should also be advanced actively. The Buddha have taught: *whatever deed brings harm for oneself, for anothers, for the both, being criticized by the learners, if one accepts it and carries it out, suffering and grief will immediately be created, such a deed is called bad one (akusalakamma) and it should be abandoned. On the contrary, whatever deed does not bring harm for oneself, for anothers and for the both, being approved by the learners, if one accepts it and carries it out, happiness and joy will immediately be created, such a deed is called good deed (kusalakamma) and it should be practised."* Confucius also had a famous sentence: *"What you do not like should not do to anothers.* "Buddhist people have to know how to react with suitable behaviour in case of facing the conflict between "selfishless" and "selfish". In the correlative life, one's happiness is closely connected with that of anothers in the community of society.

> *"Hīnaṃ dhammaṃ na seveyya.*
> *pamādena na saṃvase*
> *micchādiṭṭhim na seveyya*
> *na siyā lokavaḍḍhano."* (Dhp. v.167).

[Do not follow ignoble ways; do not live in negligence; do not embrace wrong views; do not be the one to prolong saṃsāra.]

Out of ten kinds of *Akusalakamma* (evil deeds), the four belonging to man's speech is the most difficult to avoid. So it is said that *"The person who can control his mouth can keep his mind"* and if mind can be checked, wrong physical acts can naturally be warded off. In *M.II Ambalaṭṭhikā Rāhulovāda sutta No.XII,* the Buddha used four simple and vivid illustrations to the novice Rāhula *"Should not tell a lie even for a joke."* In *M.I, Ariyapariyesana Sutta No. XXVII,* the Buddha has taught his Bhikkhus that *"whenever assembling there are two things you ought to do, that is, either discussing the Dhamma or keeping the silence of the Saints."*

In the ten *Kusalakamma,* each thing will certainly bring benefits, which should be daily practised by the Buddhists. However some appear more suitable to monks such as practising medition, expounding the doctrine, but *dāna* (charity), *veyyāvacca* (service) are more easier to laymen. Two urgent duties that Bhikkhus as well as laymen should diligently practise are *Dhammadesana* and keeping *Sīla* in life.

Through section 3---*Dhamma* as *Budhavacana,* we have clearly known the benefits being brought from listening the *Dhamma*.

Sīla or Morality is the foundation of the holy life. As the tree exists on the earth, the earth is their support.

Similarly, *Sīla* stands as the moral support of the moral activities. Why is it? Because *Sīla* has as its characteristic that it is the basis of all good qualities.[20] The practice of thirty-seven Factors of Enlightenment is on the basement of *Sīla*. As the architect of a city, when he wants to build one, first he has to prepare the foundation freed from all the stumps and thorny brakes, and then makes it level. And only then on that base, he builds the city. Similarly, the recluse develop in himself all good qualities by means of virtue, on the basis of virtue.

Morality of the Eightfold path, namely right speech, right action and right livelihood, is called "Genuine or Natural morality" (*Pakatisīla*), as distinguished from the external rules for monks or laymen the so-called "prescribed morality"*(Paṇṇattisīla)*.

If expressed in details, *Sīla* manifests itself in the form of practice of *Pañcasīla, Aṭṭhasīla, Dasasīla* and *Catu-pārisuddhisīla*.

Pañcasīla, refers to the five types of basic moral principles which are invariably observed by the householders and monks inspring for a virtuous life. They are the refraining from killing, refraining from stealing, refraining from committing adulting, refraining from telling lie, and refraining from taking intoxicating drinks.

These five principles are for all the devotees, *upasakas, upasikas* follow Eight moral principles *(Aṭṭhasīla)* in *Uposatha* days. A monk specially a novice follows ten moral principles technically known as *Dasasīla*.

The four kinds of morality consisting of purification *(Catu- pārisuddhi-sīla)* are special for monkhood namely; *Pātimokkha-saṃvara sīla; indriyasaṃvarasīla; ājīvapārisuddhisīla and paccayasannissita sīla.*[21]

20. T.W. Rhys Davids, The Questions of King Millnda,-Book I,p.52
21. Bhikkhu Ñyānamoli, The Path of Purification (Visuddhimagga), vol. I para No 42,p.16.

Pātimokkhasaṃvara means Restraint with regard to the monks' discipline code. There are 227 precepts for monks and 311 precepts for nuns. The monk trains himself in the rules he has taken upon him, perceiving danger even in the least offences.

Indriyasaṃvarasīla, restraint of the senses, whenever the monk perceives a form with the eye, a sound with the tongue...he neither adheres to the appearance as a whole, nor to its parts. He strives to ward off the attachment towards them. He watches over his senses, restrains the senses.

Ājīva-pārisuddhisīla, Purification of Livelihood. It consists therein that the monk doesnot acquire his livelihood in a way unbefitting to a monk.

Paccaya-sannissita-sīla, morality with regards to the four Requisites. It consists therein that the monk is guided by the right mental attitude when making use of the four requisites, robes, almsfood, dwelling and medicine.

As the border of a piece of rice-field, *Sīla* prevents water from overflowing. As a rampart at a country's frontier is carefully protected both inside and outside. Similar is the protection to body, speech and mind from the attack of its enemy, *akusalakamma* (evil deeds).

4.2 Akusalakamma should be won by Kusalakamma.

"Conquer the angry one by loving-kindness; conquer the wicked by goodness; conquer the stingly by generosity, and the liar by speaking the truth."

(Dhp. v.223)

And in verse 5 the Buddha also delivered: *"Hatred is indeed, never appeased by hatred in this world. It is appeased only by loving-kindness. This is an Ancient Law "*

This idea has been realized by Asoka-the Emperor of great India in ancient time. After a long period of conquest, Asoka Emperor found out that insteads of swords, *Dhamma* should be spread and overcome everywhere. Because to him, "religious conquest *(Dhammavijaya)* is the best conquest. So he condemned the slaughter of animals; he wanted people to cultivate moral virtues, such as the observance of truth, restraint, kindness, charity, purity, gentleness, generous to servants and slaves, respect, obedience to one's elders and teachers, liberality to friends, kinsmen, acquaintances. He also set free prinsoners from his prisons from time to time. He went on religious tours insteads of going on hunting for fun. He performed pious acts such as planting trees, digging wells, opening hospitals for men and beasts, in his own land and in the lands of his neighbours, too.

He had his *Dhamma* carved on rocks and stone pillars and delivered to different far places with intention to make it known by the large and to bring benefits for all.

The concept of *Dhamma* to *Asoka* king is identical with *Sīla*, morality, virtue,ethics. As T.W. Rhys Davids said "Good form" for laymen to do and to be.

"A man may conquer a million men in battle but one who conquers himself is, indeed, the greatest of conquerors" (Dhp.v.103)

4.3 The Nature of Dhamma:

Terms *"Dhamma"* and *"Adhamma"* remind us of the nature of *Dhamma* of the Buddha. In the *Alagaddūpama sutta, M.I No XXII,* the Buddha have likened his *Dhamma* as a raft. After using it to safety cross over to the other side of a river, the raft should be left behind. *"Even so,monks, is the parable of the Raft Dhamma taught by me for crossing over, not for retaining. You, monks, by understanding the Parable of the Raft, should get rid even of right Dhammas, all the more of wrong ones"* (Kullūpamaṃ vo bhikkhave ājānantehi dhammā pivo pahātabbā pag-eva-adhammā).

In relative respects, there are right and wrong, good and bad, *dhamma* and *adhamma*, but in the ultimate sense, both right and wrong, good and bad, *dhamma* and *adhamma* is conditioned by causes. Its true nature is unreal, *sūnya* or empty.

It is the same case of *Sīla*. When the society being disturbed by crimes, such as thefts, robberies, policemen are needed. But supposing that all the people are completely good, there is no need of such men. So *sīla* as policemen is used to guard our mind from evil deeds. When a man cultivated with all qualities as his characteristics, at that time his every gestures are in harmony with *Sīla*.

In brief, for the topic of *Kusala* and *Akusalakamma* we should remember words of the Buddha in verse 281.

"One should be careful in speech, be well-restrained in mind, and physically, too, one should do no evil, one should purify these three courses of action and accomplish the practice of the path of Eight Constituents made known by the Buddha."

4.4. Dhamma as Practice.

In verses 168 and 169 *Dhamma* is understood as "practice."

> *"Uttiṭṭhe nappamajjeyya*
> ***Dhammaṃ** sucaritaṃ care*
> ***dhammacārī** sukhaṃ seti*
> *asmiṃ loke paramhi ca". (Dhp.v. 168)*

[Do not neglect the duty of going on alms-round; observe proper practice (in going on alms round). One who observes proper practice lives happily both in this world and in the next.]

> *"**Dhammaṃ** care sucaritaṃ*
> *na naṃ duccaritam care*

***dhammacārī** sukhaṃ seti*

asmiṃ loke parammhi ca." (Dhp.v. 169)

[Observe proper practice (in going on alms round), do not observe improper practice. One who observes proper practice lives happlily both in this world and in the next.]

"Dhammaṃ sucaritṃ" means proper practice, in opposite of *"Dhammaṃ duccaritaṃ"*, improper pratice. The commentary says that here proper practice means stopping for alms food at one house after another in the course of the alms-round except where it is not proper to go such as courtesan's house.[22]

Go round for alms is a pre-Buddhistic tradition. It is evident that after leaving *Kapilavatthu, Bodhisattvā Gotama* has daily gone round for alms for living. And king *Bimbīsara* the first time, through his palace's window, being attracted by Gotama's serene posture when the latter was going round for alms in *Rājagaha*. After enlightenment one year, the Buddha and his disciples went home to visit his father-king *Suddhodana*. The king innocently thought *Gotama Buddha*, who was his own son, would go to no other place, but would surely come to his palace for alms- food the next day; so he did not specifically invite the Buddha.

However he already gave order to prepare food for the assembly. The Buddha, due to no invitation, went round for alms with his retinue in the city. The king, panicked and annoyed, reproached the Buddha for making a disgrace to the royal *Khattiya* family Whereupon the Buddha calmly replied that *"it was the manner of all the past Buddhas"*---to go round for alms-food from house to house, and therefore it was right and proper for him to keep up the tradition. It is in this case the two above verses have been uttered.

22. Daw Mya Tin, The Dhammapada, P.64, verse 168, fn.2

This really is a "practice" like "practice of meditation", because the practitioner has to struggle with himself to keep on practice. We should not consider it easy to follow. Because to someone with high self-respect and self-love, who have had a high social status like *Siddhattha* and royal nobilities such as *Devadatta, Nandā, Ānanda,*...or ones of Brahmin families like *Sāriputta, Moggallāna, Mahākassppa* etc. surely that it is not for their belly to go round for alms when they had left behind their family with wealth and fame. It is for purpose of searching the way out of the circle of rebirths for people and for oneself, they have to endure ascetic-lives.

We should not value this "begging food"as an action of ignobleness and laziness, although there also have this kind of persons among the *Saṅgha.* As understood by monks, the meaning and purpose of this practice can be explained as follows:

-Firstly it is to provide food for a monk to maintain his life, getting him off the worries and attachments of the world. All his time will be devoted to learning and pondering over Scriptures and to practising meditation.

-Secondly, going round for alms is helpful for him to depress and destroy his conceit *(māna).* He is practising to get rid of his self-love.

-Thirdly, the monk is the "field of merit" for people to practise their charity, with which they will be "selfishless" instead of "selfish". Getting food from them is giving them a chance to serve the Saṅgha as well as the Triple-Gem.

The image of monk in yellow-robe calmly holding the bowl reminds people of the image of the Buddha and Buddha's teachings, awaking them from the darkness of mundane life.

The proper way for going round for alms is passing from house to house. Why it is so? Because all the Buddhas love beings equally. The Buddha loves *Upāli* in the same way as that of *Rāhula*-his own son.

To return the merits of donors, the monk has duties:

-Teaching *Dhamma* and leading them on the righteous way of liberation.

-Secondly the monk himself is a symbol of morality by keeping *Sīla*. People love him and follow his example.

Each individual is a cell of the entire body of *Tathāgata*. A person leading the righteous life who even only lives without doing anything else, has directly contributed his part to purify the totalily, not to tell of actively helping others to follow the Buddha's teachings. Therefore the practice of going round for alms is venerable, appreciated by all the Buddhas in the past as well as in the future. just as the *Gotama Buddha* has said: *"Do not neglect the duty of going on alms-round; observe proper practice (in going on alms-round). One who observes proper practice lives happily both in this world and in the next"*.

4.5 Dhamma as Nature of Things.

The nature of things are qualities and characteristics, physical,mental and spiritual, which naturally belong to a person or thing. Dhamma in verse 46 has got that meaning:

"Phenūpamaṃ kāyamimaṃ viditvā
marīcidhammaṃ abhisambudhāno
chetvāna mārassa pappupphakāni
adassanaṃ maccurājassa gacche."

Marīcidhammaṃ : (marīci+dhamma) lit., mirage+nature; nature of a mirage, ie., insubstantial like a mirage.

[One who knows that this body is impermanent like froth, and comprehends that it is insubstantial as a mirage, will cut the flowers of *Māra* (i.e., the three kinds of *vaṭṭa* or rounds), and pass out of sight of the king of Death.]

The nautre of this body is impermanent like froth and insubstantial as a mirage. It also is the nature of all universal phenomena.

It impresses the characteristics of ceaselessly changing and non- self, so sufferings as result being followed.

SECTION 5

DHAMMA AS PHENOMENA

Besides the four above mentioned, the term *"Dhamma"* has also got the concept of things or world of phenomena in verses No 109, 353, 273 and 279.

5.1 Conditioned and unconditioned things.

All universal phenomena can be grouped into two types: Conditioned things *(Sankhāra)* and unconditioned thing *(Nibbāna)*.

Conditioned things are *dhammas* formed by the union of causes. It can be understood as *Sankhāra*. As the Buddha taught, "Whatever is subject to the condition of origination is subject also to the condition of cessation". Due to *cakkhu* (eye) and *rūpa* (visible form), therefore Cakkhuviññāṇa (eye-consciousness) arises. Due to *sota* (ear) and *sadda* (audible objects), there is *Sotaviññāṇa* (ear- consciousness) and so on. Due to the existence of five *khandhas,* there is the existence of a human-being. And all *dhammā* formed by the union of causes are named conditioned things.

Unconditioned thing is *Nibbāna,* which is a state "unborn, unoriginated, uncreated and unformed" constrasting with the born, originated, created and formed phenomenal world.

The term *"dhamma"* used in the sense of both conditioned and unconditioned states of life are in verses 273 and 279

"Sabbe ***dhammā*** *anattā" ti*

Yadā puññāya passati

Atha nibbindati dukkhe

Esa maggo visuddhiyā? (Dhp. v. 279)

[All phenomena *(dhammas)* are without "self"; when one sees this with insight wisdom, one becomes weary of *dukkha* (i.e, the *khandhas*). This is the path of purity.]. In the two previous verses 277 and 278;

"Sabbe sankhārā aniccā" ti....

"Sabbe sankhārā dukkhā" ti.....

The term *"sankhārā"* here is applied to any conditioned things. while in the third verse the term *"dhamma"* is used in the sense of both conditioned and unconditioned things (as interpreted by *Nārada Thera* in his *Dhammapada* book, verse 279).

5.2 Realms of Conditioned Things.

According to Buddhism, Realms of conditioned things are three which are sub-divided into thirty-one in number, namely:

-*Kāmāvacaraloka* : Sentient Existence: 11

-*Rūpāvacaraloka*: Realms of Form : 16

-*Arūpāvacaraloka*: Realms of Formless: 4

If divided according to kinds of being, the thirty-one realms can be enumerated into six. They are:

1. *Niraya:* Woeful states.

2. *Peta yoni:* The place of Petas or ghost beings.

3. *Tiracchāna yoni*: The realm of animal.

4. *Asura yoni:* The place of Asura demons.

5. *Manussa* : Human realm.

6. *Devas:* The realms of Gods.

In general, the six realms may be divided into two groups, the first four of which is relatively miserable due to unwholesome *kamma (Duggati)* and the other relatively fortunate due to wholesome *kamma (Sugati)*.

Let us have a general look at each of these realms individually and starting from the realm at the bottom, *Niraya*.

There are various hells in Buddhism and they are principally eight hot hells and cold hells. In the hells, beings suffer incalculable and inexpressible pain due to their past evil deeds. When these *kamma* are exhausted, they are reborn in a more fortunate realm of existence.

The next realm is the realm of ghosts *(petayoni)*. Petas are not spirits or mere disembodied souls. They possess ugly or deformed bodies of varying imagnitude. The *Petavatthu* book deals with the stories of those unfortunate beings. They in this realm suffer chiefly from hunger and thirst, and from heat and cold. They are completly bereft of the objects of their desire.

Tiracchāna yoni-the realm of animal, the living beings suffer from the fear and pain due to constantly killing and eating one another. They also suffer from fear and pain caused by ṃan killing them for food, skin, bone or horns. Even if they are not killed, domestic animals are forced to work for man and are driven on by hooks and whips. All these is a source of suffering.

The realm of *Asura* demons are *Asurayoni*. Peter D. Santina refers them as demi-gods. They are more powerful physically and are more intelligent mentally than human beings. Yet they suffer because of jealousy and conflict. It is said that their special characters are anger, envy and jealousy.

I am going to skip the realm of human beings for a while and go on the realm of gods *(Devas)* which is the happiest among the six realms:

There are three kinds of gods:

-gods of *kāmāvacara* loka.

-gods of *Rūpāvacaraloka* and

-gods of *Arūpāvacaraloka*.

Gods of *kāmāvacara loka* are six in number-namely,

-*Cātummahārājika*- the realm of the four kings who are the guardian deities of the four quarters of the firmanent.

-*Tāvatiṃsa*-the realm of the thirty three *Devas*. The *Deva Sakka* is the chief of this realm.

-*Yāma*- the realm of the *Yāma Devas*.

-*Tusita*-the realm of Delight.

The *Bodhisattvas* who have perfected the *Pāramitās* reside in this plane until the suitable moment comes for them to appear in the human realm to attain Buddhahood. The *Bodhisatta Metteyya*, the future Buddha, at present residing in this realm.

-*Nimmānarati*-the realm of the *Devas* who rejoice in their own creations and,

-*Paranimmita vasavatti*-the realm of the Devas who make others' creation serve their own ends.[23]

The first four realm of woe, ghost-beings. animal, *Asura* and *manussa* and six kinds of gods of *kāmāvacara loka* belong to *Kāmāvacaraloka*. The remaining two *Rūpāvacaraloka* and *Arūpāvacaraloka* are realms of gods.

Gods of *Rūpāv*. and *Arūpāv*. are those who cultivate meditation and attained meditative absorptions *(Jhānas)*. As result of this good *kamma*, when dying they were born in these correspondent realm to enjoy their merits until its exhausting.

We have had a general view of five realms of woe, ghosts, animal, *Asura* demons and gods. These five realms express two extremes: One is great pain and another great happiness. Contrasted with the agony of hell with boiled oil and hot fire, hunger, thirst, heat, cold, fear, pain, anger of the first four realms is the realm of great pleasures of heavens. In the woe, beings

---

23. Nārada Thera, the Buddha- Dhamma, New Delhi, Asian Educational Services, 1991, p.200.

due to dull character covered with greed, hatred and delusion, it really hard for them to digest and enjoy the taste of *Dhamma*. In heavens, the happiness of sensual pleasures or spiritual pleasures have been lasting a long period of time. Beings here rarely face the impermanence of birth, old age, sickness and death, so most of them getting deep attachment in enjoying their merits, forget to practise the *Dhamma*. When suddenly comes the impermanence of old- age and death, they have no chance to ponder over the Truth.

In *Manussa* or human-realm, beings also suffer unhappiness as the Buddha often remind us *"Life is full of sufferings"*, but it won't go to the extreme unbearable agony like the first four. Life is also full of pleasures which most of beings like to grasp with, however it won't go to the extreme happiness as the realm of gods. And the life span is neither too long nor too short, being enough for men to recognize three marks of existences. Besides, in this realm, beings get more chances to meet Buddhas themselves and to listen to and practise the Dhamma, because *Bodhisattvas* often choose this realm to develop *pāramitās* or for the last life to fulfil their bodhi to attain Buddhahood. In addition to that, beings of human-realm possess enough knowledge to understand the noble meanings of *Dhamma* to practise in life. Because of these reasons, the Buddha have often insisted that human-realm is the best among all six ones. Being born as human-being is difficult, being listened to the noble *Dhamma* is much more difficult!

"Suppose the whole world were a vast ocean, and on the surface of this ocean there were a yoke floating about, blown about by the wind, and suppose at the bottom of the ocean there lived a blind tortoise which came to the surface of the ocean once every hundred years. Just as difficult as it would be for that tortoise to place its neck through the opening in that yoke floating about in the ocean, just so difficult is it to attain opportune birth as a human being!"

"Khōo thay, d*uoc lām nguoi,*
Khõ thay, duoc sõñg cõn,
Khõ thay, nghe dieu phāp,
Khõ thay, Phāt ra dõi."

[Hard to gain is birth as man; hard is life of morals; hard to get is the opportunity of hearing the *Ariyadhamma;* hard it is for a Buddha to appear]

(Dhp. v. 182)

It is possible for us to interpret that these six realms are the different states of psychology in the same person. It also is expressed that the six realms are present here, in this world. These interpretations are not quite unreasonable, because the states of agony, anger envy, jealousy, fear, happiness, serenity are states of mind everyone can absolutely perceive in his daily life. It also is the realm of woe that can be seen in prisons; the misery of persons being harassed just like animal; men due to feud, envy, hatred killed one another, just like scene in *Asura* realm. All of these are obvious here, in this very life of man- society. However, if we insist that besides the human-realm and animal-realm, there is no four others of hell, ghost, *asura* and gods, it may be a certain mistake!

The Buddha has confirmed the long course existences of beings through His exclamation:

"Long I endure the circles of rebirth,
Seeking but finding not the architect,
Rebirth continual is continual pain..."

5.3 Cause of formation of Realms : Paṭiccasamuppāda.

What is the cause to circle men in the six realms? In order to explain the formation of men and of the world, the Buddha has delivered the sermon of Paṭiccasamuppāda-the Law of Dependent Origination.

Before and during the time of the Buddha, the philosophical atmosphere of India was clouded with many metaphysical theories. Generally, it belongs to two extreme attitudes such as Eternalism and Annihilationism. While the Upanisadic tradition denied change and impermanence as being illusory and upheld the reality of a permanent "self", the materialist tradition considered matter to be ultimately real, there is no after life. These two extreme attitudes are rejected by the Buddha in the doctrine *Paṭiccasamuppāda* or more popularly, as the *Nidāna* Chain, or Law of Dependent Origination. The doctrine expresses that all physical and psychical phenomena are conditioned by antecedent physical or psychical factors, and that whole of existence can be shown to be an uninterrupted flux of phenomena.

The general formula sets out in the early discourse, as follows:

"When this is present, that comes to be,

From the arising of this, that arises.

When this is absent, that does not come to be;

On the cessation of this, that ceases."

(Imasmim sati idam hoti, Imassa uppādā idam uppajjati. Imasmim asati idam na hoti; Imassa nirodhā idam nirujjhati].

The classical formule of the doctrine sets out in twelve links which run as follows:

"With ignorance *(Avijjā)* as condition, there are volitional activities *(Sankhāra)*.

With volitional activities as condition, consciousness *(viññāṇa)*.

With consciousness as condition, mentality-materiality *(nāma- rūpa)*.

With mentality-materiality as condition, the sixfold base (*salāyatana*) with the sixfold base as condition, contact (*phassa*).

With contact as condition, feeling *(vedanā)*

With feeling as condition, craving *(taṇhā)*

With craving as condition, clinging *(upādāna)*.

With clinging as condition, becoming *(bhava)*

With becoming as condition, birth *(Jāti)*

With birth as condition, there is ageing and death *(Jarāmaraṇa)* and sorrow, lamentation, pain, grief, and despair; thus there is the arising of this whole mass of suffering".

There are various ways to interpret the Law of Dependent Origination. One way to understand it is over a period of three life-time: the past life, the present life and the future life. In this case, ignorance and mental activities belong to the past. The next eight components of dependent origination--- *Viññāṇa, nāmarūpa, salāyatana, phassa, vedanā, taṇhā, upādāna* and *bhava* belong to the present life. And the last two *Jāti* and *Jarāmaraṇa* belong to the future life. To the presence, *Avijjā* and *Sankhāra* are causes, the next eight components are their results; to the future, the eight components are causes and the last two are their fruits.

There also are scholars who interpreted it as follows:

Due to *Avijjā* and *Sankhāra* which are deeds created in the past that *Viññāṇa* is formed to seek rebirth. The process of rebirth is explained as the combining of two factors, *Viññāṇa* and *Nāma-rūpa* from which the foetus is formed in the mother's womb and the beginning of a new life-span is represented.

When the individual is born, his senses *(Salāyatana)*, if they are not impaired, will start functioning. In the process, *Phassa* and *Vedanā* and *Taṇhā* are formed. *Taṇhā* is the cause of *Upādāna*, as a result of which the process of becoming *(Bhava)* is set in motion. This stage represents again the end of a life span and the begining of a fresh one. Birth as the result of becoming. Birth, then, is considered as the cause of the entire mass of suffering that one is faced with in his life.

The third interpretation is authoritative too. It divides the twelve components into three groups, and these are defilements *(Kilesa)*, actions *(Kamma)*, and sufferings *(Dukkha)*. According to this scheme, *Avijjā*, *Taṇhā* and *Upādāna* belong to the group of defilements. *Sankhāra* and *Bhava* belong to the group of actions. The remaining seven, that is, *Viññāṇa*, *Nāma-rūpa*, *Salāyatana*, *Phassa*, *Vedanā*, *Jāti* and *Jarāmarana* belong to the group of sufferings.

We have the defilements which may be described as impurities of the mind-*Avijjā*, *Taṇhā* and *Upādāna*. These mental impurities result in actions, actions done in previous lives *(Sankhāra)* and actions that we perform in this life *(Bhava)*. Together, these defilements and these actions result in rebirth. In other words, they result in the formulation of consciousness, the name and form, six senses, in contact, in feeling, in rebirth, and in old-age and death. In this interpretation three defilements and two actions are causes of rebirth and sufferings. Rebirth and sufferings are their effects. In this sense, the twelve components of dependent-origination present a picture of *Saṃsāra* with its causes and its effects. When the twelve links are at work, the process of life and death continues. When there is the stop of these links, there is no continuity of the cycle of birth and death.

How the process of repeated existence comes to an end? It comes to an end by breaking any of the chain. It means when there is no ignorance, there is no volitional forces*(sankhāra)* and so on. And the complete path for freedom is the Noble Eightfold Path.

"Maggānaṭṭhaṅgiko seṭṭho,
Saccānaṃ caturo padā
Virāgo seṭṭho dhammānaṃ
Dvipadānañca Cakkhumā." (Dhp. 273)

[Of path, the path of Eight Constituents is the noblest; of Truths, the Four Noble Truths are the noblest; of the dhammas, the absence of craving (i.e.*Nibbāna)* is the noblest; of the two-legged beings, the All Seeing Buddha is the noblest].

Nibbāna will be discussed in the last section.

SECTION 6

DHAMMA AS BODHIPAKKHIYA DHAMMA

(37 Factors of Englightenment)

Now we come to the next concept of *Dhamma* named *Bodhipakkhiya Dhamma*, the path of virtue or thirty seven Factors of Englightenment. They are so-called because they are principles which are conducive Enlightenment.

We have found this concept through verses No 44, 45, 79, 86, 164, and 364.

"Ko imaṃ paṭhaviṃ vicessati
Yamalokañca imaṃ sadevakaṃ
Ko dhammapadaṃ sudesitaṃ
Kusalo pupphamiva pacessati" (Dhp.v. 44)

[Who shall examine this earth (i.e. this body) of the world of *yama* (i.e.the four lower worlds) and the world of men together with the world of *devas*? Who shall examine the well-taught Path of Virtue (*Dhammapada*) as an expert florist picks and chooses flowers?]

"Sekho pathaviṃ vicessati....sadevakaṃ
Sekho dhammapadaṃ sudesitaṃ....pacessati." (Dhp.v. 45)

[The *Ariyasekha* shall examine this earth....The *Ariyasekha* shall examine the well-taught Path of Virtue.....]

Dhammapadaṃ sudesitaṃ=the well taught Path of Virtue, here means the thirty-seven Factors of Enlightenment *(Bodhipakkhiya- Dhamma)*.

*"Sekho"*or *"Sekhapuggala"*, that means one who is practising the *Dhamma*, and has entered the path, but has not yet become an *Arahanta*. The term is applied to the first seven *Ariyapuggalas*, the eight or *Arahat* being *Asekha*.[24]

Verses 44 and 45 were uttered on the occasion of five hundred *Bhikkhus* who after a journey, in their leisure of that evening they had an idle talk, especially the condition of the land they have passed. The Buddha came to them. After knowing the subject of their talk, he advised them not to have gossip with the external world, but they should concentrate on their own body.

A man is a composing of *Nāma* and *Rūpa*. Earth, water, fire and air are four basic elements of *Rūpa*. For summarily, the Buddha mentioned *Paṭhaviṃ* (earth) representing for the body or *Rūpa* of man.

What should the practitioner be mindful for the subject related to his own body? That is impurity, impermanence and soullessness. Through section 5 we have known the misery of realms of hell, ghost-beings, animals and *Asura*-demons; we have recognised the temporary pleasures of the realms of gods and finally, we have confirmed that it is lucky being a human-being and it is much more lucky having chance to listen to the Buddha's teachings in which the helpful way of Liberation is *Bodhipakkhiya dhamma*. As in a flower-garden, the expert-florish shall choose the most beautiful flowers to make nice corollas used in accordance with their need, similarly, among thousands of worldy objects, life- span shorten with the time passing-by, the intelligent one shall race against the impermanence, not to waste time for gossip, they choose for themselves suitable objects to ponder over and by the way of practising thirty-seven Factors of Enlightenment to strive for Liberation.

---

24. Op. cit: 18, verse 44, fn.1

The Buddha repeatedly impressed its importance and the advantage one must achieve by following it through verses 86, 79 and 364.

"Ye ca kho sammadakkhāte.
dhamme dhammānuvattino
te janā pāramessanti
maccudheyyaṃ suduttaraṃ"(Dhp.v.86)

[Few among men reach the other shore *(Nibbāna)*; all the others only run up and down on this shore[25], but those who practise according to the well-expounded *Dhamma* will reach the other shore, having passed the realm of Death (i.e.,*Saṃsāra)*, very difficult as it is to cross.]

Or in verse 79:

"Dhammapīti *sukhaṃ seti*
vippasannena cetasā
ariyappavedite ***dhamme***
sadā ramati paṇḍito."

[He who drinks in the *Dhamma*, lives happily with a serene mind; the wise man always takes delight in the *Dhamma(Bodhipakkhiya Dhamma)* expounded by the Noble Ones *(Ariyas)*]

The term *Dhamma* in *"Dhammapīti"* refers to the Buddha's teachings.

"Dhammārāmo dhammarato
dhammaṃ *anuvicintayaṃ*
dhammaṃ *anussaraṃ bhikkhu*
saddhammā *na parihāyati (Dhp. v. 364)*

[The bhikkhu, who abides in the *Dhamma* who delights in the *Dhamma*, who meditates on the *Dhamma*, and is ever mindful of the *Dhamma*, does not fall away from the *Dhamma* of the virtuous].

25. Translation of verse 85 with the meaning connected with that of verse 86.

The first four "*Dhamma*" here refer to the Buddha's teachings while *Saddhammā*, the *Dhamma* of the virtuous, means the thirty-seven Factors of Enlightenment and the Nine Transcendentals (*Lokuttara Dhamma.*)[26]

The term *Dhamma* in "*Ariyānaṁ Dhammajīvinaṃ*" of verse 164 translated as "Noble Ones (*Ariyas*) who live according to the *Dhamma*"... The term *Dhamma* here can be understood either as the Buddha's teachings in general or *Bodhipakkhiya Dhamma* in particular.

Bodhipakkhiya Dhamma is practical method for appling in Buddhists' daily life. It is from simple to complex to suit with any level of characteristics. Because of its speciality, we will here, by turn, discuss about some aspects of its formation and a critical study of it is needed.

6.1 The formation of the concept:

The entire Buddha's teachings of practices and principles are composed in thirty-seven "*Dhammas*", i.e. *Bodhipakkhiya Dhamma*, 37 Factors of Enlightenment.

The *Pāli* word *Bodhipakkhiya* is probably derived from the *Sanskrit* form "*Bodhipaksyā dharmāḥ,*" which was the earlier of the two (Bodhi+paksya/paksa), as this word does not often occur in the *Nikāyas* or the *Milindapañha*, though all the factors are mentioned in the *Mahāparinibbāna- sutta*. As E. Hardy has pointed out, the collective term *Bodhipakṣā dharmāḥ* is found in the *Lalitavistara* (86.182.11). It also occurs in the *Mahāvastu* (II, 290.6). The term emphatically refers to *bodhi* and not to the *Nirvāṇa* of the *Pāli* scriptures. Both the term and the complete formula seem to have originated among the *Sanskritists* or *quasi- Sanskritists*, who were the fore-runners of the *Mahāyāna*.

The number "thirty-seven" is first mentioned in the *Saddharmapuṇḍarīka*, but *cata-sāhaṣrikā prajñāpāramitā*, the

26. Op.cit.p. 125, verse 364, fn.1

list is given more than thirty-seven *Dharmas*. (The numeral "thirty-seven", however, is also found in the same book). The *Pāli Nettipakaraṇa*, which dates from the beginning of the Christian era, mentions forty three *Dharmas*. *Asvaghosa* mentions only twenty-eight items in the *Saund-kāvya* (XVII,24, ff), and he does not use the term *Bodhipaksya*.[27]

The formula, in its final form, includes the following thirty- seven *Dharmas*, which are usually given in this order:

Four *Satipaṭṭhāna (Smṛty-upasthānāni)*	4
Four *Sammappadhāna (Samyak-prahāṇāni)*	4
Four *Iddhipāda (Ṛddhi-pādāḥ)*	4
Five *Indriya (Indrlyāṇi)*	5
Five *Bala (Balāni)*	5
Seven *Bojjhanga (Bodhy-aṅgāni)*	7
Aṭṭangikamagga (Āry-āṣṭ-āṅga- mārgaḥ)	8
Total:	37

6.2 A Study of Bodhipakkhiya Dhamma

(1) Four *Satipaṭṭhāna* (Fields of Mindfulness)

There is this one way, monks, for the purification of beings, for the overcoming of sorrows and griefs, for the going down of sufferings and miseries, for winning the right path, for realising *Nibbāna*, that is to say, the four Fields of Mindfulness."

It is Buddha's statement when starting to preach *Satipaṭṭhāna sutta* to His *Bhikkhus*.

Why?

Because *"Sati"* is like a door-keeper at the mind door. As a door-keeper remains standing at the door, so long he is quite alert the undesirable person is unable to enter the room. Similarly, when there is the presence

27. Har Dayal, The Bodhisattva doctrine in Buddhist Sanskrit Literature, India, Shantilal jain, Shri Jainendra Press, 1978, p.81,82

of awareness or mindfulness at mind-door, there is no occasion for appearance of the immoral states.

The practice of *Satipaṭṭhāna* is a fourfold namely:

Kāya-satipaṭṭhāna (Mindfulness of the Body).

Vedanā-satipaṭṭhāna (Mindfulness of Feelings)

Citta-satipaṭṭhāna (Mindfulness of Consciousness)

Dhammā-satipaṭṭhāna. (Mindfulness of Phenomena)

"Herein, monks, a monk fares along contemplating the body in the body, ardent, clearly conscious (of it), mindful (of it) so as to control the covetousness and dejection in the world; he fares along contemplating the feelings in the feelings ; ardent, clearly conscious (of them), mindful (of them) so as to control the covetousness and dejection in the world; he fares along contemplating the mind in the mind, ardent, clearly conscious (of it), mindful (of it) so as to control the covetousness and dejection in the world; he fares along contemplating the mental objects in the mental objects, ardent, clearly conscious (of them), mindful (of them) so as to control the covetousness and dejection in the world."

And how, monks, does a monk fare along contemplating the body in the body?

KĀYA-SATIPAṬṬHĀNA :---

It means analysing and observing the body or contemplation to the body or mindfulness as regards the body.

There is a whole Sutta devoted to this subject named *Kāyagatāsatisuttaṃ* (M.No.xix.) Through this *Sutta,* one can practise mindfulness of the body in the ways as follow:

-One practises *Ānāpānasati* with four subjects of the body in which one observes the natural process of breathing in and breathing out in every moment. During the time, he has to draw his mind from different subjects and fixed it on the in-coming and out going breaths. His mind is alert, all time, his mind is aware of the in-coming and out-going breaths. By this way, his mind becomes pure and tranquil.

In another way one observes the physical movements such as sitting, standing, walking, lying etc. He has to be aware of his movements. For instance, if a man is walking, at that time he is fully conscious of his walking. Similarly, when he is sitting, he is full aware of his sitting.

Or one contemplates the loathesome character of our body which is nothing beside the heap of 32 types of impurities namely hair, nails, teeth, skin etc. By this practice one cannot find in his bofy anything for which he can develop the pride.

Or one observes in personality of man that it is composed of *nāma* (mind) and *rūpa* (form) which is nothing beside four elements: *Paṭhavī,Āpo, Tejo* and *Vāyodhātu* (viz.earth, water, fire and air respectively).

Or one sees the corpes of the persons who died one, two, three, four or five days before. As he observes them in different stages of decomposition, he reflects to his own body which cannot escape from this condition and fells detachment from it.

While he is thus diligent, ardent, self-resolute, those memories and aspirations that are worldy are got rid of; by getting rid of them the mind itself is inwardly settled, calmed, focussed, concentrated. Thus, does a monk develop mindfulness of body.

VEDANĀ-SATIPAṬṬHĀNA:

Here one contemplates the three types of feeling. They are:

1. *Sukhā vedanā* 2. *Dukkhā vedanā and* 3. *Upekkhā vedanā.*

Sukhā vedanā means pleasant feeling which is divided into two groups:

-Sukhā vedanā : physical pleasant feeling and,- *Somanassā vedanā*:mental pleasant feeling.

Dukkhā vedanā means unpleasant feeling which is also divided into two: *-Dukkhā vedanā:* physical unpleasant feeling and, *Domanassā vedanā*: mental unpleasant feeling.

Upekkhā vedanā means indifferent feeling. It is of only one type, that is neutral mental feeling.

Thus the five types of feeling used to appear in various moments. The practitioner remains mindful in the moment of anything of particular type of feeling.

CITA-SATIPṬṬHĀNA :

Here one practises Mindfulness with regard to *Citta*. He knows the nature of mind is fickle, restless, unsteady like a monkey or a wind. One observes his mind that it is composed of *Lobha* (greed), *Dosa* (hatred) and *Moha* (Delusion), then he tries to destroy all these defilements. Or it is composed of *Alobha* (Sacrifice), *Adosa* (friendliness) and *Amoha* (Right understanding), then he cultivates all of these qualities.

DAMMĀ-SATIPAṬṬHĀNA:

In this process, one ponders over the various *dhammas* namely:

-Pañcanīvaraṇāni : five hindrances.

-pañcakkhandhā : five aggregates.

-Satta bojjhaṅgā : seven enlightenment factors.

-Dvādasāyatāni : twelve bases, and,

-Cattarāriyasaccāni : four Noble Truths.

He considers them and understands them clearly.

These four *Sati* of *Kāya, Vedanā, Citta* and *Dhammā* are *Catu Satipaṭṭhāna*. Among them, Kāyasatipaṭṭhāna is the most important because it is easy to practise, and being suitable to any level of characters.

As the Buddha declared in *Kāyagatāsati-suttaṃ* that if *Kāyagātasati* being developed, made much of, making it a vehicle, making it a foundation, practising it, increasing it, and fully undertaking it, then one certainly gets ten advantages. They are , he is one who overcomes dislike and liking; fear and dread; can bear physical unpleasant feelings; acquires the four meditations and can experience the various forms of psychic power.

And if one probably develops *Satipaṭṭhāna* either for seven years, or it's no need for seven years, just for six years, five years, four, three, two, one or even seven months, six, five...., or even seven days only, one of two fruits is to be expected for him: either profound knowledge here-now, or, if there is any residuum remaining, the state of non-returning.

It is in this reason the Buddha has taught:

"There is this only way, for the purification of beings, for the overcoming of sorrows and griefs, for the going down of sufferings and miseries, for winning the right path, for realising Nibbāna, that is to say, the four Fields of Mindfulness."

This kind of practice these days is popularly approved in Japan and Vietnam in monasteries and among Buddhist lay-people.

(2) Four Sammappadhāna : (Right Efforts)

In the ceaseless struggle between good and bad, moral and immoral, one seeks the help from the Four Right Efforts. The Buddha taught it in various ways, the best-known being the efforts to avoid, overcome, develop and maintain. They are:

-Preventing the arising of ill, unprofitable states not yet arisen. (avoidance).

-As to ill, unprofitable states that have arisen, he puts forth desire to destroy them (overcoming).

-As to profitable states that have not yet arisen, he puts forth desire for their arising (developing)

-As to profitable states that have already arisen, he puts forth desire, makes an effort for their continuance, for their non-confusion, for their more-becoming, increase, culture and fulfilment (maintaining)(S.V. trans,p.8)

Why are these efforts named Right Efforts?

That means a balanced effort neither too weak nor too strong. It can be illustrated with the story of *Soṇa Kolivisa* in *Aṅguttara Nikāya III* (trans.p.266).

While the Ven. *Soṇa* lived alone and secluded in *Coolwood* near *Rājagaha,* this thought occured to him: "Of those disciples of the Blessed One who are energetic, I am one." (He had been born in a rich family and had tender feet. After ordination he practised walking meditation with so much effort that his meditation-walk was stained with blood from his cracket feet, hence these reflections). "yet my mind is not detached and free of the cankers....Would it not be better for me to give up the training, return to the lower state of a lay-person, enjoy my riches and do good deeds?"

The Buddha knew in his mind *Soṇa's* thoughts. He went to him and asked him. " Tell me, *Soṇa,* when in earlier days you lived at home, were you not skilled in playing the lute's stringed music?" "Yes, Lord". "And tell me, Soṇa, when the strings of your lute were too taut, was your lute then tuneful and playable?"Certainly not, Lord" "And when the lute-strings were too lack, was your lute then tuneful and playable? "certainly not, Lord". But when your lute-strings were neither too taut nor too slack, but in the middle-pitch, was your lute then tuneful and playable? "Certainly, Lord". In the same way, *Soṇa,* if effort is applied too strongly it will lead to restlessness, if too slack it will lead to lassitude. Therefore, keep your effort balanced, penetrate to a balance of the faculties".

"Just as, monks, the river Ganges flows to the east, slides to the east, tends to the east, even so a monk, by cultivating the four right efforts, making much of the four right efforts, flows, slides and tends to *Nibbāna*." (S.V.ch.I.p.219)

(3) Four Iddhipāda ; (Bases of Psychic Powers)

This term consists of two words: Iddhi and Pāda. Various translations were made, usually "Bases of psychic powers." But to Har Dayal, the best translation of the term *"Iddhi"* is "wonder-working-power" and of *"Pāda"* is base. So *Iddhipāda* is translated "Bases of wonder-working power."[28]

Iddhipāda is of four:

---The basis of psychic powers of which the features are *desire,* together with the co-factors of concentration and struggle.

---The basis of psychic powers of which the features are *energy* together with the co-factors of concentration and struggle.

---The basis of............. are *thought*............ and struggle

---The basis of psychic power of which the features are *investigation,* together with the co-factors of concentration and struggle.

If, by emphasizing *desire,* a monk lays hold of concentration, lays hold of one pointedness of mind, this act is called *"desire-concentration."*

If, by emphasizing *energy,* a monk lays hold of concentration, lays hold of one-pointedness of mind, this act is called *"energy-concentration."*

28. Ibid: 105

If, by emphasizing *thought*, a monk..., this act is called *"thought-concentration."* Now, if by emphasizing investigation, a monk...., this act is called *"investigation-concentration."*

For the non-arising of ill, the abandoning of ill, the arising of profitable states and the establishing the profitable states, if a monk generates desire and makes an effort, sets going energy, these are called *"The co-factors of struggling."*

This desire and this desire-concentration and these co-factors of struggle are called by one name: *"The basis of psychic power of which the features are desire, together with the co-factors of concentration and struggle."*

The same are three others.[29]

The Buddha taught that these bases of psychic power, if cultivated and made much of, conduce to going neither to the hither nor to the further shore, i.e, going strainght to *Nibbāna*. Why it is so?

Because they have powers to cut off all ill, to fulfil comprehension, and wisdom. When a monk has cultivated and made much of the four bases of psychic power, he enjoys manifold forms of psychic power: he gets six *Abhiññā* (super- knowledges). Furthermore, whosoever has cultivated and fully undertaken them, if he so wished, he might remain on earth for his full span of life, or for what is left of it. It is by the fact of cultivating and making much of these four bases fo psychic power that the *Tathāgata* is called *"Arahant, a Fully Enlightened One."*

(4) Pañca Indriyāni and Pañca Balāni. (Faculties and Forces):

Buddhism or the path of the Buddha, is the path of purification. In this path, it has been repeatedly told

---

29. Saṁyutta-nikāya V, Book VII, trans.p.239

that for gradual purification, the practice of five *Indriyas* and five *Balas* are needed. They are:

Saddhā, Viriya, Sati, Samādhi, Paññā and,

Saddhābala, Viriya-bala, Sati-bala, Samādhi-bala, and *Paññā-bala.*

Various translations have been made for the term *Pañca Indriya*. The familar one is " Five Faculties". but to Har Dayal, the term *indriya* means *"belonging to the ruler", "governing ruling, controlling, principle, directive force."* "These five *indriyas* are related to moral and spiritiual qualities and values"(Pāli Dict.). So it should be rendered as "Five chief categories" or "chief controlling principles".

Pañcabalāni means Five Forces.

The final formula of these two have passed a process of change and selection. The *Pāli* texts speak of four, five or seven *balas*, and the name vary. Only three items (*Viriya, Samādhi* and *Paññā*) are mentioned at *Mahāvastu* and *Samādhi* is ommitted at *Lalitavistara. Chanda* (Strong desire) takes the place of *Saddhā* in several passages of *Lalitavistara*.

There five *Indriyas* and *Balas* are mentioned as a group in *Saṁyutta nikāya V* and in several passages of Buddhist Sanskrit literature. H.Kern thinks that the only different between the *Indriyas* and the *balas* is that the later are more intense than the former. But to Har Dayal the *Indriyas* are regarded as static in character, while the *Balas* are dynamic.

A brief discussion of each of them is given belows:

SADDHINDRIYAṂ ; (SADDHĀ+INDRIYAṂ).

Saddhā means "Faith". We have known that Buddhism is the religion of wisdom. The Buddha is a representative of wisdom, being a great leader who always gives much respect to the individual's judgement. He has honestly advised the people of *Kālāmas* of *Kesaputta* not to accept anything merely on the authority of another, but to exercise their own reasoning and judge for themselves whether anything is right or wrong. Thus, is *Saddhā-indriya* here a blind-faith?

---Absolutely not. *Saddhā* here is accompanied with *Paññā*. After considering carefully, we have found out that if we follow and pratise the teachings of the Buddha, we ourselves, not anyone else, will gain much advantage first. For this reason it is said that *"Saddhā is mother of all kinds of merit."*

Milindapañha gives two characteristics of Saddhā:

"Sampasādana lakkhaṇā Saddhā" and *"Sampakkhandanalakkhaṇā Saddhā"*.

When we find the definition *Sampasādanalakkhaṇa Saddhā*, it means that *Saddhā* has the characteristic of Tranquillisation. Just as when water becomes dirty and water- purifying-gem *(udakappasādako maṇi)* is put into it, immediately the dirt particles disappears and the water becomes pure. Similarly, when consciousness becomes dirty with hindrances, *Saddhā* makes it clear, serene and untroubled.

It is again said that *Saddhā* has got the characteristic of aspiration-*Sampakkhandhana lakkhaṇā saddhā*. The *Yogāvacara* establishing himself in *Saddhā* makes right efforts for higher achievement. He becomes *Sotāpañña* again proceeds further and he becomes *Sakadāgāmi*, *Anāgāmi* and *Arahatta* in due course. In this way *Saddhā* insprires one to proceed further for attainment of gradual purification and higher states.

VIRIYINDRIYA: (VIRIYA+INDRIYA)

The literal meaning of the word *Viriya* is energy, perseverance. We have discussed it in part (2) Four *Sammappadhāna*. Here we just add one characteristic of it which *Milindapañha* mentioned is *"mental moral support."* All the good qualities which it supports do not fall away. This has been explained with the help of illustration.

Sometimes due to the heavy rain or the push of strong wind, the thatch starts falling. The house owner erects a wooden pillar and provides supports accordingly. Getting support in this way, the thatch of the house does not fall. Similarly when there is the downfall the consciousness due to immoral forces, *Viriya* comes to help and grant support and make the mind strong.

SATINDRIYA : SATI+INDRIYA)

We have known the important role of *Sati* (Mindfulness) at Part 1- --*Catu satipaṭṭhāna*, and its necessity to monks on the way towards freedom of rebirths.

Two characteristics are hereby mentioned such as:

---*Apilāpana lakkhaṇā Sati* and,

---*Upagaṇhanā lakkhaṇā Sati*.

When we say *Apilāpana lakkhaṇā Sati*, it means that *Sati* has the characteristic of *repetition*. And how is repetition the mark of mindfulness?

---"As mindfulness, O king, springs up in his heart, he repeats over the good and evil, right and wrong, slight and important, dark and light qualities, and those that resemble them, saying to himself. "These are four *Satipaṭṭhāna*, these the four *Sammappadhāna*, these four *Iddhipāda*..., this serenity and this insight, this wisdom and this emancipation." Thus does the recluse follow after those qualities that are desirable, and not after those are not; thus does he cultivates those which ought to be practised, and not those which ought not. That is how repetition is the mark of mindfulness."

Again *"Upagaṇhanā"* is defined as *Sati's* characteristic—*Upagaṇhanā lakkhaṇā sati*. It means that Sati has the characteristic of "keeping up", to make us aware of the fact that we have so many *dhammas* in us which are helpful and so many which are not helpful. Doing so, it inspires us to acquire developing the *dhammas* which are helpful and give up the *dhammas* which are not helpful.

It has also been explained with the simile of the adviser of the king. As theking has an adviser who everyday tells or advises the king about the useful and harmful dhammas. Knowing them so, the king makes the evil in himself die out, and keeps up the good. Similarly, with the development of *Sati* one is conscious of his good qualities.

---SAMĀDHI INDRIYA

---PAÑÑĀ INDRIYA

Will be discussed in the next chapter.

(5) Seven Bodhyangāni. (Bojjhanga)

[Seven factors or constituents of Enlightenment]

Seven *Bojjhanga,* seven constituents of Enlightenment, which forms Bodhi. Bodhi is derived from the root *"budh"* meaning Knowledge, Enlightenment, and therefore, the knowledge possesed by the Enlightened One, the Buddha. It is considered as being attainable through the accomplishment of the principles conductive to the maturing of Enlightenment.

Seven *Bojjhanga* are:

-*Sati* (mindfulness).

-*Dhamma-vicaya* (investigation of the Buddha's teachings)

-*Viriya* (Energy).

-Pīti (Joy).

-*Passaddhi* (Serenity).

-*Samādhi* (Concentration) and

-*Upekkhā* (Equanimity).

We have above mentioned *Sati* and *Viriya. Samādhi* will be discussed in the next chapter. Thus here we will discuss only four constituents of *Dhammavicaya, Pīti, Passaddhi* and *Upekkhā.*

-DHAMMA-VICAYA:

Vicaya (Skt. *pravicaya*) means investigation. *Dhamma* here means Buddha's teachings. So *Dhamma-vicaya* means investigation of the Doctrine.

On the way leading to the highest goal of life, the knowledge of Buddha's teachings is an essential constituent to construct the Bodhi. Because *"practice without learning is a blind practice; well-versed without practice is a bookcase."* However, as above mentioned, Ch'an of China found by *Bodhidharma,* whose policy is much prefered practice to theory, even Buddha's image. This way is suitable to the minor kind of person with high character, who has accumulated the seed of *Bodhi* from incalculable past existences. To this kind of person, he is able to get enlightened at once even hearing only one verse, such as the sixth patriarch *Hue Nang* of Ch'an of China. Besides, almost human-beings covered with deep delusion, they have to cultivate their mind from time to time by pondering over the teachings of the Lord.

-PĪTI: is zest, joy or pleasurable interest. It is derived from $\sqrt{'pi'}$. It is a psychic factor, the function of which is to make psychic factors and consciousness full of joy. It is a kind of inner joy while *Sukha* is the happiness got through body when the object is realized. It has been explained with a simile.

Suppose there is a man who is travelling through the desert. After travelling for some days, he becomes extremely tired. There is no food to eat, no water to drink. Being suppressed in this way he looses the hope of life. In the meantime he catches a sigh a man coming from the opposite direction. His cloth is wet, water is dropping down from his hair. The traveller thinks that there must be a tank nearby. His mind is now full of joy (Pīti). He with this hope comes up to the tank little later. Drinking water as much as he likes and becomes satisfied. It is the state of *Sukha* but *Sukha* is attained with the objectives realized.

Pīti is one of five *Jhānaṅga,* antidote of *Vyāpāda* (ill-will or hatred), one of five *Nīvarana* (hindrances), being practised thoroughly at *Rūpājhāna* stage. Nārada Thera in his *"A Manual of Abhidhamma"* mentioned five kinds of *Pīti.*

PASSADDHI:

Passaddhi is composed of Pa + $\sqrt{sambh}$, to calm, to be tranquil. Passadhi is tranquillity, calmness, quietude, serenity.

The chief characteristic of *Passaddhi* is the suppression or the allaying of feverishness of passions *(Kilesa daratha vūpasama).* It is like the cool shade of a tree to a person affected by the sun's heat. *Passaddhi* is opposed to uddhacca, restlessness or excitement. When highly developed it becomes a factor of Englightenment.

There are two kinds of *Passaddhi,* viz. *Kāya-passaddhi* and *Citta-passaddhi.* Here *Kāya* is refered to the body of psychic factors-namely, *Vedanā, Saññā* and *Saṅkhāra.* And *Citta* connotes the whole consciousness.[30]

UPEKKHĀ:

'Upa' means impartially, justly + $\sqrt{ikkh}$, to see, to view, to look *(ikkhati),* literally means seeing impartially. It is viewing an object with a balanced mind, neither with attachment nor with aversion. *Aṭṭhasālinī* states: *"This is impartiality in connection with the object, and implies a discriminative knowledge."*

Here *Upekkhā* does not mean mere neutral feeling, but a state of mind without attachment to good and bad situations, to agreeable and disagreeable matters.

Nārada Mahāthera mentions four kinds of *Upekkhā* accompanied different kinds of *Citta.*[31] *Visuddhimagga*

---

30. Nārada Thera, A Manual of Abhidhamma, Srilanka, The Colombo Apothecaries, 1980, p.110
31. Ibid: 53,54

enumerates ten kinds of *Upekkhā* (The Path of Purity, Vol.II, p.184-186).

Upekkhā is one of *Brahmavihāra. Buddhaghosa* gives a very appropriate simile in illustrations of the four divine states in which *Upekkhā* has the promotion of the aspect of neutrality as its characteristic, like the mother's attitude to the son who busies himself with his own affairs.

Upekkhā and *Ekaggatā* are important factors of the fourth *Jhāna* of *Rūpajjhāna* and of the whole four stages of *Arūpajjhāna*.

How about the practice of seven *Bojjhanga?*

When a monk, dwelling aloof, remembers and turns over in his mind the teaching of the Norm, it is then that the limb of wisdom which is mindfulness is established in that monk. When he cultivates the limb of wisdom which is mindfulness, then it is that the monk's culture of it comes to perfection. Thus he, dwelling mindful, with full recognition investigates and applies insight to that teaching of the Norm and comes to close scrutiny of it.

With that way he proceeds into the practice of Norm-investigation *(Dhamma-vicaya)* and so on.[32]

Finally the Buddha declared seven fruits the practitioner can get when the seven limbs of wisdom are thus cultivated, thus made much of. The highest is *Arahattaphala* and the lowest is *Sotāpattiphala*.

(6) The Eightfold Path. (Aṭṭhaṅgikamagga).

Buddha says there is suffering in this universe. Suffering arises due to certain cause. Cessation of this suffering is Nirvāṇa and the path is nothing but the Eightfold path, namely:

---

32. Saṁyutta Nikāya V, trans. p. 55-57

-*Sammādiṭṭhi*	(Right View)	PAÑÑĀ
-*Sammāsankappo*	(Right Thought)	
-*Samāvācā*	(Right Speech)	SĪLA
-*Sammā kammanto*	(Right action)	
-*Sammā ājīvo*	(Right Livelihood)	
-*Sammā vāyāmo.*	(Right Effort)	SAMĀDHI
-*Sammā sati.*	(Right Mindfulness)	
-*Sammā samādhi.*	(Right Concentration)	

This Eightfold Path is a complete path for freedom. When a man follows this properly, he gradually gets purity. In the end he realizes the goal of life, technically called *Nibbāna*.

The entire teaching for practice of the Buddha is not beyond thirty-seven constituents of Enlightenment. One follows one group of it properly, he can end up his circle of rebirth, not to say of he follows to practise the entire thirty-seven. So again we remember what the Buddha said:

"Those who practise according to the well-expounded Dhamma (Samma-dakkhāte dhamme dhammānuvattino)[33] *will reach the other shore (Nibbāna), having passed the realm of Death (i.e., saṃsāra), very difficult as it is to cross."*

Although the entire Buddha's teachings of practices are composed in thirty-seven *Bodhipakkhiya Dhamma*, it generally is not beyond *Sīla-Samādhi* and *Paññā*.

In *Aṭṭhaṅgikamagga*, *Sammā-diṭṭhi* and *Sammā sankap-po* belong to PAÑÑĀ. *Sammā- vācā*, *Sammā-kammanto* and *Sammā-ājīvo* belong to SĪLA. And the last three, *Sammā-vāyāmo*, *Sammā-sati* and *Sammā samādhi* belong to SAMĀDHI. Sometimes *Sammā Vāyāmo* is classified into

33. Sammadakkhāte dhamme dhammānuvattino [Samma + akkhāte = well-preached Anuvattino = According to.]

Sīla, because Right Effort is needed in any state of mind.

It seems that there are three separated divisions *Sīla, Samādhi* and *Paññā* but each of three functions without separation with the other two. When a person is practising *Sīla,* that means at the same time there is the appearance of *Samādhi* and *Paññā* in him. The same way is applied to *Samādhi* and *Paññā.*

In 37 *Bodhipakkhiya Dhammas,* the four *Satipaṭṭhāna* and four *Iddhipāda* belong to *Samādhi.* Four *Sammappadhāna* is identical with Right Effort which belongs to either *Samādhi* or *Sīla. Pañca Indriyāni* and *Pañca-Balāni* are composed in *Samādhi* and *Paññā.*

Sīla has been discussed in section-4. In the next part *Samādhi* and *Paññā* will be related.

SECTION 7

DHAMMA AS SAMATHA AND VIPASSANĀ

Besides various concepts the term *Dhamma* has conveyed, a special one we should really notice is that of *"Dvayesu Dhammesu,"* the only term appeared in verse 384 of the *Dhammapada* refering to Two *Dhammas*, that is, the practice of Tranquillity *(Samatha)* and Insight Meditation *(Vipassanā)*.

"Yadā dvayesu ***dhammesu***
Pāragū hoti brāhmaṇo
Atthassa sabbe saṁyogā
Atthaṃ gacchanti jānato". (Dhp. v. 384)

[When the *Brāhmana* is well-established in the two *Dhammas*, then, in that knowing one, all fetters are destroyed].

By the *Satipaṭṭhānasutta*, the Buddha has repeatedly emphasized that "this is the only way for the purification of beings, for the overcoming of sorrows and griefs, for the going down of sufferings and miseries, for winning the right path, for realising Nibbāna, that is to say, the four Fields of Mindfulness."

This attitude of the Buddha stated that meditation is the only path leading to freedom. And the thirty-seven Factors of Enlightenment which is made short in Eightfold-path is the only way being practised through Meditation.

Before coming to the main points to discuss, some confusion about the words Mindfulness, Meditation,

Concentration and Contemplation may be arisen. And what are they?

7.1. Distinction: Mindfulness, Meditation, Concentra tion and Contemplation.

Mindfulness *(Sati)* means analysing and observing an object, awareness of the presence of object as a door-keeper at mind-door. There are four kinds of *Sati* we have discussed.

Contemplation as watchfulness would, therefore, not much differ from Mindfulness (Sati), as both are essentially kinds of observation.

Meditation [Skt. *Dhyāna*, Pāli *Jhāna*, Chinese *Chan*, and Japanese *Zen*], too, is a form of attention and reflection. Its basic meaning is meditation, absorption, abstraction and trance. The use of term may have been pre-Buddhist. There are two spheres of *Jhāna* namely:

-*Rūpajjhāna* (or *Rūpavacara-jhāna*), the fine material sphere.

-*Arūpajjhāna* (or *Arūpavacara-jhāna*), the immaterial sphere.

When we say *Dhyāna*, that is chiefly used to refer to the four meditative absorptions of *Rūpajjhāna*. There are four states (or five, according to *Abhidhamma*) in *Rūpajjhāna*. There are numerous methods and subjects of meditation. (Buddhaghosa mentioned forty *kammaṭṭhāna*, objects of meditation). The practice of *Dhyāna* leads to *Samādhi* (Concentration) due to the development of one-pointedness (*Ekaggatā*).

Concentration, then, is called "the power of individualizing", developed by practice, for it focusses the attention on one point, whereby distracting influen-ces are kept at a distance. This is the checking of the five hindrances, when full estasy *(Jhāna)* may occure, which is truly right concentration *(Sammāsamādhi)*.

Kammaṭṭhāna such as *kāyagatāsati*, *Ānāpanasati*, *Anussati* (recollections) such as recollection of the virtues of the Buddha, recollection of the Dhamma, of the Saṅgha.....or contemplation of a device as a clay disk *(paṭhavī-kasiṇamandala)* are forms of meditation or mental development *(Bhāvanā)*.

7.2. Samatha-bhāvanā-Samādhi

In the process of practising meditation, as its result, one's mind is developed and the mental development is called *Bhāvanā*. Here one has to distinguish two kinds:

* Development of Tranquillity *(Samatha-bhāvanā)*, i.e., Concentration *(Samādhi)* and,

* Development of Insight *(Vipassanā-bhāvanā)*, i.e., wisdom *(Paññā)*.

If we stop thinking, our mind only concentrate to follow either the breath in and out or a single object (such as earth- *kasiṇa*....) with vigilance and clear consciousness, that is called *Samatha-bhāvanā*.

If our mind is following an object, analyzing and pondering over it, although this object is either our breath or five hindrances, five aggregates, four elements, seven *Bojjhanga*....such activity is named *Vipassanā-bhāvanā*.

The way of practice of the Four *Satipaṭṭhāna* is composed both *Samatha* and *Vipassanā*. Concentrating the mind on the objects of *Kāya*, *Vedanā*, *Citta* and *Dhamma* is *Samatha*, and pondering over the true characteristic-impermanences and soullessness of them, is *Vipassanā*.

By means of deeply practising *Samatha*, *Yogāvacara* will attain the state of concentration *(Samādhi)* by destructing five hindrances which are substituted by the five *Jhānaṅgas*. He from time to time perceives in his mind the five meditative absorption stages of *Rūpaloka* and the four stages of *Arūpaloka*.

Due to skilfully practising *Vipassanā, Paññā* is disclosed. With *Paññā,* one clearly sees the true conditioned nature of all things. Now he is fed up with worldly pleasures, detachment from them and in due course cutting of all defilements.

Why it is so?

Because Concentration has got non-distraction as its characteristic. Its function is to eliminate distraction. It is manifested as non-wavering.[34]

Milinda-Pañhā, mentioned "being the leader" as its characteristic. All good qualities have meditation as their chief, they incline to it, lead up towards it, and are as so many slopes up the side of the mountain of meditation.

If being not practised, Concentration often very weak-is one of the seven mental states *(Sabbacitta sādhāranā cetasika)* inseparably associated with all consciousness.

Right concentration *(Sammā-samādhi),* as the last link of the Eightfold Path is defined as the four meditative Absorptions *(Jhāna).* In a wider sense, comprising also much weaker states of concentration, it is associated with all *kusala* consciousness. Opposite to *Sammā-samādhi* is *Micchā-samādhi*-wrong concentration associated with all karmically unwholesome consciousness. However as always, every time Concentration is mentioned, that means it conveys the meaning of *Sammā- samādhi.*

In Concentration one distinguishes three grades of intensity:

(1) "Preparatory concentration" *(Parikamma-samādhi)* existing at the beginning of the mental exercise.

34. Buddhaghosa, The Path of Purification (Visuddhimagga), Trans. by Bhikkhu Ñyānamoli, p.85

(2) "Neighbourhood concentration" *(Upacāra-samādhi)* i.e., concentration "approaching" but not yet attaining the Ist *Rūpajjhāna.*

(3) "Attainment Concentration" *(Appanā-samādhi),* i.e. concentration which is present during four stages of *Jhāna.*

Concentration of saints of *Lokuttara* stage, i.e., four *Maggas* and four *Phalas* is called supramundane *(Lokuttara),* having *Nibbāna* as object. Any other concentration even that of *Rūpajjhāna* stages and *Arūpajhāna* stages, is merely mundane *(Lokiya).* Buddhaghosa in his *Visuddhimagga* divided Concentration into five kinds. If going into details with sub- divisions, there are altogether sixteen kinds of concentration.[35]

According D. 33, the development of concentration *(Samādhi- bhāvanā)* may procure a fourfold blessing:

(1) Present happiness through the four absorptions.

(2) Knowledge and vision *(Ñāna-dassana)* here probably identical with the divine Eye.

(3) Mindfulness and clear comprehension through the clear knowledge of the arising, persisting and vanishing of feelings, perceptions and thoughts.

(4) Extinction of all cankers *(āsavakkhaya)* through understanding the arising and passing away of the five aggregates.

Tranquillity, or Concentration of Mind, according to *Sankhepavaṇṇana* (Commentary to *Abhidhammattha Saṅgaha),* bestows a threefold blessing: favourable rebirth, present happy life, and purity of Mind which is the condition of Insight.

7.3 Vipassanā-bhāvanā-Paññā

Insight meditation or Development of Insight *(Vipassanā- Bhāvanā)* leads to wisdom *(Paññā).*

---

35. Ibid: 85,86

Paññā = Pa + ñā (Pa means Rightly; Ñā, to Know).

Paññā, literally, means right knowing. It is generally translated as understanding, knowledge, wisdom or insight. It helps us knowing the *dhamma* as they really are. When we understand the nature of *dhamma* perfectly we become able to give up which that are not beneficial and to acquire which that are beneficial. Therefore it has been defined as *"Chedana Lakkhaṇā Paññā"* which means it has the characteristic of cutting down or destroying all the cankers. And enlightenment is also its mark *(Obhāsana Lakkhaṇā Paññā)*. When wisdom springs up in the heart, it dispels the darkness of ignorance, it causes one seeing things as they really are in the light of *Aniccā, Dukkha* and *Anattā*.

As *Paññā* dominates in understanding the real nature and as it overcomes ignorance, it is called a controlling faculty *(indriya)*.

It is wisdom that is the decisive liberating factor, it has to be mostly discovered through the process of trainings of the two others *Sīla* and *Samādhi*. The culmination of wisdom practice leads directly to the stages of Holiness.

With regard to the condition of its arising one distinguishes three kinds of knowledge: Knowledge based on Learning *(Suta- mayā-paññā)*; knowledge based on Thinking *(Cintā-mayā-paññā)* and knowledge based on Mental Development *(Bhāvanā-mayā-paññā)*.

"Knowledge Based on Learning" is that knowledge which one has heard from others and thus acquired through learning.

"Knowledge Based on Thinking" is that knowledge which one has acquired through one's own thinking, without having learnt it from others. And,

"Knowledge Based on Mental Development" is that knowledge which one has acquired through mental development in this or that way; and which has reached the stage of Full Concentration (Vis. XIV).

The first and second are "Reasoning" *(yoniso manasikāra)*, while the last is wisdom *(Paññā)*.

Wisdom may be either mundane (*Lokiya*, the first and second), or supramundane (*Lokuttara*, the third). Supramundane wisdom is of three kinds:

1. Joined with one of the four supramundane Paths *(Maggas)*.

2. Joined with one of the four Fruitions of these paths *(Phalas)*.

3. Regarding the Extinction of Consciousness *(Nirodha- samāpatti)*.

There are altogether twelve types of wisdom composing into four groups as mentioned in *Visuddhimagga XIV*. *Milindapañha* noted the comprehension is the characteristic mark of reasoning while "cutting off" is that of wisdom. Just as the barley reapers with the left hand they grasp the barley into a bunch, and taking the sickle into the right hand, they cut it off. In the same way, the recluse by his thinking grasp his mind, and by his wisdom cut off his failings.

Buddhism is the religion of wisdom, the instinctive insight. The Buddha required his disciples to see thing with wisdom. By wisdom men cut off *Nīvaraṇa*-defilements of mind, root out greed, hatred and delusion and finally obtain *Nirvāṇa*.

In brief, "Concentration" *(Samādhi)* is the indispensable foundation and precondition of Insight by purifying the mind from the 5 mental defilements or hindrances *(nīvaraṇa)*, while Insight *(Vipassanā)* produces the four supramundane stage of Holiness *(Lokuttaravacāra)* and deliverance of mind.

All these do not mean that one has to follow *Samatha* first and *Vipassanā* in the second step. Or someone prefer to practise either one of them. The best way is practising both depending on his state of mind. If his mind is excited with greed or hatred or distraction, finding no peace for meditation, the best way in this situation is *Samatha* to calm down the mind. With peaceful mind, if he finds out that his characteristic tends to sensual desire, in this case the contemplation of the loathesome character of the body with 32 types of impurities, or mindfulness on different states of decomposition of corpses is the best. If his characteristic tends to hatred, the practice of *Mettā* (Loving-kindness) in this case is needed. He comtemplates all kinds of sufferings that human beings suffer in the sickness, diseases and death as displayed daily in hospital to arise *Mettā*. Or he ponders over the deep-rooted delusion beings have accumulated from their incalculable past existences, from which their characters differ one anothers to arise *Mettā*. Or he regards all beings as relatives due to the long course of *Saṃsāra* to arise *Mettā*. This is he is using the opposited method.

Going to further stage, he directs his mind to ponder over the Four Noble Truths, the conditioned state of *Dhamma* in the light of the Law of Dependent-Origination, through it he recognises the danger of *Taṇhā*, the emptiness, unreality, temporariness of *Dhammas*. With this knowledge he develops detachment from them. He, being in mundance but supramundane, unties the grasping of sense-organs, worldly objects, consciousness, breaking off the chain of twelve links to enter the door of freedom.

Nāgasena Thera mentioned twenty-eight good qualities of meditation. It will give the practitioner long life, and endow him with power, it cleanses him from faults, it removes from him any bad reputation giving him a good name, it destroys discontent in him filling him with content, it releases him from all fear endowing him with confidence, it removes sloth far from filling him with zeal, it takes away lust and ill-will and dullness, it puts an end to pride, it breaks down all doubt, it makes his heart to be at peace, it softens his mind, it makes him glad, it makes him grave, it gains him much advantage, it makes him worthy of reverence, it fills him with joy, it fills him with delight, it shows him the transitory nature of all compound things, it puts an end to rebirths and finally it obtains for him all the benefits of renunciation.

There are four reasons for which the *Tathāgatas* devote themselves to meditation after Enlightenment. They are: They may dwell at ease,- and on account of the abundance of the advantages of meditation,- and on account of its being the road to all noble things without exception-and because it has been praised and lauded and exalted and magnified by all the Buddhas.[36]

The Buddha therefore says, "May you develop mental concentration, O monks; for whoso is mentally concentrated, sees things according to reality. And in Milindapañha it is said: "Just as when a lighted lamp is brough into a dark chamber, the lamp- light will destroy the darkness and produce and spread the light, just so will Insight once arisen, destroy the darkness of Ignorance and produce the light of knowledge."

Dhammapada said, *"When the Brāhmaṇa is well-established in the two Dhammas, then, in that knowing one, all fetters are destroyed."*

36. T.W. Rhys. Davids, the Questions of King Milinda, Book I, p. 197,198

SECTION 8

DHAMMA AS NINE TRANSCENDENTALS (4 Maggas + 4 Phalas + Nirvāṇa)

Besides all the concepts mentioned above, the term *Dhamma* also refers to the sense of Nine Transcendentals which means four *Maggas*, four *Phalas* and *Nirvāṇa* in verses 115, 217, 261 and 393. This is the highest stages the *yogāvacara* attained by means of diligently going through *Samatha-bhāvanā* and *Vipassanā-bhāvanā*.

> *"Yo ca vassasataṃ jīve*
> *apassaṃ* ***dhammamuttamaṃ***
> *ekāhaṃ jīvitaṃ seyyo*
> *passato* ***dhammamuttamaṃ****"* *(Dhp. v. 115)*

[Better than a hundred years in the life of a person who does not comprehend the noble *Dhamma*, is a day in the life of one who comprehends the Noble *Dhamma*].

Dhammamuttamaṃ = The Noble *Dhamma* or the Highest *Dhamma* (The Nine Transcendentals)[37]

The path on which a *Bodhisattva* has to undertake is practising 37 *Bodhipakkhiya Dhamma*, cultivating ten *Pāramitās* along with ten stages of *Bhūmi* to develop *Bodhicitta* which is consisted of both *Sūnya* (or *prajñā*) and *Karuṇā* (compassion). This *Bodhicitta* as being of the nature of "pure truth, pure, evolving from the voidness of all phenomena, fulfilling Buddhahood, good in every respect, beneficial to beings, produce the thought of

---

37. Daw Mya Tin, The Dhammapada, Verse 115, p. 43, fn.2

Enlightenment, practice leading to Enlightenment". This *Bodhicitta* is his object to practise.

Similarly, the path on which an *Arahanta* has to pass is practising *Sīla-Samādhi-Paññā* through 37 *Bodhipakkhiya Dhamma*. To him, Meditation is the only means, supramundane *Paññā* is what to achieve and *Arahanta phala* is the fruit to be attained.

Before entering into the *Arahantaphala*, the *yogāvacara* has to pass all stages of meditative absorptions of *Rūpajjhāna* and *Arūpajjhāna*, then comes *Lokuttara* stages of Saints. Correspondent to each stage of *Jhāna* is an aspect of consciousness *(Citta)*. So all the aspects of consciuosness can be orderly grouped into four types according to degree of development: *Kāmāvacaracitta*, *Rūpāvacaracitta*, *Arūpāvacaracitta* and *Lokuttaracitta*.

8.1 The process to attain Rūpajjhāna stages:

A man is living in the world of desire that means he is in *Kāmāvacara* stage. Due to his accumulated merits, or after vicissitudes of life, a desire to get rid of the circle of rebirths arising in him. He left family, leading a homeless life, following the Buddha's steps, eager to put himself under the control of *Sīla*:

He trains himself with modesty and fear of blame. His bodily conduct, his conduct in speech, in thought, his mode of living, he keeps all these under control, perfectly pure. He guards six doors of sense-organs towards forms, sounds, smells, tastes, touch and mental objects. He is moderate in eating, being intent on vigilance and possessed of mindfulness and clear consciousness. Until then he is practising and perfecting his conduct *(Sīla)*.

Now going further, he develops meditation to destroy five hindrances *(nīvaraṇas)* namely:

Kāmacchanda,

Vyāpāda,

Thīnamiddha,
Uddhaccakukkucca and,
Vicikicchā.

Kāmacchanda means strong desire for sensual pleasure of *indriyas* to beautiful objects.

Vyāpāda means ill-will or a desire to harm others.

Thīnamiddha generally is sloth and torpor, technically means Idleness. This is the state of dull witted, half-conscious, sleepy.

Uddhaccakukkucca-uddhacca means distractions, and *kukkucca* means brooding over. In this way, brooding over what has been done and what has not been done is *kukkucca*. In general sense, worry and flurry are the *uddhaccakukkucca*. Or there arises continuously different mental states one after one in his mind and he can't stop them to concentrate on one object. This is the state of *uddhaccakukkucca*.

Vicikicchā means doubt regarding to the Buddha, Dhamma and Saṅgha. He feels doubt about the method of practising meditation, he wonders whether it is the right path to bring peace and meditative absorptions. It is a state of *vicikicchā*.

The antidote of five Nīvaraṇas is the five *Jhānaṅga* namely: *Vitakka, Vicāra, Pīti, Sukha* and *Ekaggatā,*

Vītakka means steadily keeping the mind towards the object, while *Vicāra* is fixing the mind on the object. As a bee flies to a flower, after roling around the flower then he sits on it to take nectar. Flying to and rolling around the flower just like *Vitakka*. Sitting on the flower just like *Vicāra*

Pīti is a kind of inner joy while *Sukha,* a kind of bodily happiness. We have known the distinction of them with the simile of the traveller through a desert.

Ekaggatā means one-pointedness by which concentration is developed.

Through Meditation practice, one gradually substitutes five hindrances by five *Jhānaṅgas* in this way:

Vitakka destroys *Thīnamiddha; Vicāra* destroys *Vicikiccā; Pīti* to *Vyāpāda; Sukha* to *Uddhaccakukkucca* and *Ekaggatā* to *Kāmacchanda.*

As a man contracting a loan, now is freed himself from the loan; as a seriously ill man recovering from that disease; as a prisoner freed from the prison; as a slave got freedom from that slavery; and as a rich and prosperous man passed safely a wilderness of desert, they are very happy and joyful. Similarly, as a debtless man, as a healthy, as a prisoner freed, as a slave got liberty, and as a rich getting secure ground is a *Bhikkhu* after getting rid of these five hindrances.

The Buddha expressed the state of mind of a *Yogāvacara* obtained the Four Stages of *Rūpajjhāna* in *Majjhima Nikāya* I, *Mahāssapurasuttaṃ No. XXXIX* as follows:

"By getting rid of these five hindrances which are defilements of the mind and weakening to intuitive wisdom then, aloof pleasures of the senses, aloof from unskilled states of mind, he enters on and abides in the first meditation which is accompanied by initial thought *(Vitakka)* and discursive thought *(Vicāra)* is born of aloofness, and is rapturous *(Pīti)* and joyful *(Sukha).*

And again, a monk by allaying inital and discursive thought, with the mind subjectively tranquillised and fixed on one point, enters on and abides in the second meditation which is devoid of initial and discursive thought, is born of concentration and is rapturous and joyful.

And again, a monk by the fading out of rapture, dwells with equanimity, attentive and clearly conscious and experiences in his person that joy of which the *ariyans* say: "Joyful lives he who has equanimity and is mindful", and he enters on the abides in the third meditation.

And again, a monk by getting rid of joy and by getting rid of anguish, by the going down of his former pleasures and sorrows, enters on and abides in the fourth meditation which has neither anguish nor joy, and which is entirely purified by equanimity and mindfulness.

After attaining the state of fourth meditation, he, with his mind thus composed, quite purified, quite clarified, without blemish, without defilement, grown soft and workable, fixed, immovable, directs his mind to the knowledge and recollection of former habitations, the knowledge of the passing hence and arising of beings, and the knowledge of the destruction of the cankers. With the knowledge of the destruction of the cankers, he understands as it really is: This is dukkha, this is the arising of dukkha, this is the stopping of dukkha, this is the course leading to the stopping of dukkha. He understands as it really is: These are the cankers, this is the arising of the cankers, this is the stopping of the cankers, this it the course leading to the stopping of the cankers. When he knows thus, sees thus, his mind is freed from the canker of sense-pleasures, the canker of becoming and the canker of ignorance. In freedom the knowledge comes to him: "I am freed"; and he comprehends: "Destroyed is birth, brought to a close is the Brahma-faring, done is what was to be done, there is no more of being such or such."

Monks, this is called a monk who is a recluse, and who is a *brahman,* and who is washen, and who is expert in lore, and who is learned, and who is an *ariyan,* and who is a perfected one."

"Sīladassanasampannaṃ

***dhammaṭṭhaṃ** saccavedinaṃ*

attano kamma kubbānaṃ

taṃ jano kurute piyaṃ" (Dhp. 217)

[He who is endowed with Virtue and Insight, who is established in the *Dhamma,* who has realized the Truth and performs his own duties, is loved by all men].

Nikāya here mentioned the four stages of *Rūpajjāna* with the appearance of *Jhānaṅgas* as follows:

Vitakka, Vicāra, Pīti, Sukha, Ekaggatā, are prominent at the First *Jhāna.*

Pīti, Sukha, Ekaggatā at the second *Jhāna.*

Sukha and *Ekaggatā* at the Third *Jhāna.*

Upekkhā and *Ekaggatā* at the Fourth *Jhāna.*

However, *Abhidhamma* analised *Jhānaṅgas* of *Rūpāvacara* into five by putting *"Vicāra, Pīti, Sukha, Ekaggatā"* at the second *Jhāna.* All others are the same.

The second notice is that after attaining the four *Rūpajjhāna* stages, the *yogāvacara* directed his mind to practice and obtain three *Abhiññā* (supernormal powers) namely:

* *Pubbe-Nivānanussati Ñāna.* (Reminiscence of past births).

* *Dibbacakkhu.* (Celestial Eye) and,

**Āsava-ksaya-vijānana* (the knowledge of the destruction of the Āsavas). With Āsavakṣaya-vijñana he clearly understands the Four Noble Truths, absolutely cuts off all defilements to attain *Arahantaphala.*

However through *Majjihima* with suttas namely, *Ariyapariyesanasuttaṃ* (MI. No. XXVII) Alaggadūpamasuttaṃ (M.I, No. XXIII); Nivāpasuttaṃ (M.I, No. XXVI) the complete process for attaining *Arahantaphala* would run in the procedure as follows: attainment of *Rūpajjhāna,* next *Arūpajjhāna,* then six *Abhiññā* and finally Four *Maggas* and four *Phalas* of *Lokuttara* stage.

8.2 Attainment of Arūpajjhāna Stages:

After the attainment of four *Rūpajjhāna* stages, the practitioner directs his mind to practise objects without form such as *Ananta Ākāsa* (infinite space), *Ananta viññāṇa* (infinite consciousness), *Ākiñcañña* (the Nothingness of Consciousness) and "Neither perception nor non-perception." And as its result, respectively he will pass the Four *Arūpajjhānas* namely:

* *Ākāsānañcāyatana.*
* *Viññāṇañcāyatana.*
* *Ākiñcaññāyatana and,*
* *Nevasaññānāsaññāyatana.*

8.3 Attainment of Abhiññā:

After passing *Nevasaññānāsaññāyatana,* his mind is in the state of no feeling-perception concentration. With his mind thus composed, quite purified, quite clarified, without defilement, he develops the six supernormal powers *(Abhiññā)* namely:

* *Iddhividha* (Skt. *Ṛddhi*): Various psychic powers.
* *Dibbacakkhu* (Skt. *Divya-cakṣus*): Celestial Eye.
* *Dibbasota* (Skt *Divya-srotra)*: Celestial Ear.
* *Pubble-Nivāsanussati Nāna* (Skt. *Pūrva-Vivāsānusmṛti-Jñāna)*: Reminiscence of past births.
* *Paracittavijānana* (Skt *para-citta-jñāna*): Thought reading.
* *Āsava-kṣaya-vijānana* (Skt. *Āsrava-kṣaya- jñāna*): The knowledge of the destruction of the *āsavas.*

We also remember that the *yogāvacara* used to practise the Four *Iddhipāda* (Bases of psychic-powers), he will surely get these six ones.

8.4 Attainment of 8 Lokuttara stages and Nirvāṇa.

With the sharp sword of *Āsava-ksya-vijānana* he in due course cuts off the ten subtle-state-fetters *(Saṁyojanas)* namely:

1. *Sakkāyadiṭṭhi* (false view).

2. *Vicikicchā* (doubt).

3. *Sīlabbataparāmāsa* (grasping in practice of wrong rites and rituals).

4. *Kāmarāga* (delight in sensual pleasures).

5. *Paṭigha* (hatred, antipathy).

6. *Rūparāga* (desire for having existence in the *Rūpa Brahmaloka*).

7. *Arūparāga* (desire for having existence in the *Arūpa Brahmaloka*).

8. *Māna*. (Conceit).

9. *Uddhacca* (distraction).

10. *Avijjā* (ignorance).

In his first effort he tries to destroy the three first fetters namely *Sakkāyadiṭṭhi*, *Vicikicchā* and *Sīlabbataparāmāsa*. Firstly, he simply knows that they are being destroyed and he is in *Sotāpattimagga* stage. His consciousness is called *Sotāpattimagga citta*. Next, he knows that they have been destroyed. He is in *Sotāpattiphala* stage and his consciousness is called *Sotāpattiphala citta*. After destruction of these three fetters he is called *Sotāpañña* or a man entering the stream that leads to *Nirvāṇa*. He has the vision of *Nirvāṇa* at this stage.

"As the traveller by night sees landscape around him by each flash of lightning and the picture so obtained long thereafter swims before his dazzled eyes, so the individual seeker by the flashing light of Insight catches a glimpse of Nirvāṇa with such clearness that the after picture never more fades from his mind[38].

If he doesnot realize *Nibbāna* in this life he will return to life seven times more for attaining it.

38. Nārada Thera, The Buddha-Dhamma, p. 290

In his second efforts, he weakens the two *Kāmarāga* and *Paṭigha*. Firstly, he understands that they are being made weak. In the second stage he understands that they have been made weak. The former is called *Sakadāgāmimagga* and the second *Sakadāgāmiphala*. After their weakening he becomes *Sakadāgāmi* means Once-Returner. If he does not get *Nirvāṇa* in this very life, he will have to come once again to realize it.

In his third efforts he proceeds to destroy the above two fetters and gets *Anāgāmimagga* and *Anāgāmiphala* stages. Now he is *Anāgāmi,* Never Returner. If he does not realize *Nirvāṇa* in this life, he will not be returned here but born in a divine kingdom *Suddhāvāsa* from where he directs to *Nirvāṇa*.

In his fourth efforts he proceeds to destroy the remaining five fetters: *Rūparāga, Arūparāga, Māna, Uddhacca* and *Avijjā*. The highest reward for this struggle are *Arahantamagga* and *Arahanta phala*. Now his tittle is *Arahant a* worthy person, emancipated being. *"Destroyed is birth, brought to a close is the Brahma-faring, done is what was to be done, there is no more of being such or such"*.

"Yamhi saccañca **dhammo** *ca, ahiṃsā saṁyamo damo, sa ve vantamalo dhīro, "***thero***" iti pavuccati"*. (Dhp. v. 261).

[Only a wise man who comprehends the Four Noble Truths and the *Dhamma,* who is harmless and virtuous, who restrains his senses and has rid himself of moral defilements is indeed called a thera].

"Na jaṭāhi na gottena, na jaccā hoti brāhmaṇo, yamhi saccañca **dhammo** *ca, so sucī so ca brāhmaṇo"*. (dhp.v.393).

[Not by wearing matted hair, nor by lineage, nor by caste, does one become a brāhmaṇa; only he who realizes the Truth and the *Dhamma* is pure; he is a *brāhmaṇa*].

The term *"Thera"* and *"Brāhmaṇa"* here are identical with *"Arahant"*.

These are the formal steps to advance the *Arahanta* stage. However the *Nevasaññānāsaññāyatanna* is regarded as a dangerous stage by the Buddha himself in the *Aṅguttara Nikāya III*. (Because in this stage *yogāvacara's* consciousness is too weak). So in many *suttas* he suggests his disciples going straight from the Fourth *Rūpajjhāna* stage to the practice of *Abhiññā* (only three among six), especially *Āsava-ksaya-vijānana,* the knowledge of the destruction of the *āsavas*. With this *paññā* he cuts off ten fetters to get *Arahantaphala*.

There are many cases in which persons attained Arahantship straight way by merely cultivating Insight without the aid of *Jhānas*. They are named *Sukkha Vipassakas,* dry-visioned *Arahants,* who accumulated gems for Englightenment from past existences. He will never return to the circle of rebirths and finally attaining *Nirvāṇa,* a permanent peaceful state.

Nirvāṇa will be discussed in the next and also last section.

SECTION 9

DHAMMA AS THE TRUTH

Now we come to the last concept of *Dhamma* in the *Dhammapada,* that is, *Dhamma* as the Truth in verses 70,176, 205 and 354.

The common meaning of the Truth is the quality or state of being true. One expresses the truth through body, speech and mind. Doing or telling or understanding the fact as it is to appreciate the Truth. That is the meaning of *Dhamma* as used in verse 176

"Ekaṃ ***dhammaṃ*** *atītassa*
Musāvādina jantuno.
Vitiṇṇa paralokassa
Natthi pāpaṃ akāriyaṃ"

[For one who trangresses the Truth, and is given to lying, and who is unconcerned with the life hereafter, there is no evil that he dare not do.]

In verse 11, word *"Sāraṃ"* also contains the meaning of Truth such as.

"Asāre sāramatino
Sāre cāsāradassino
te ***sāraṃ*** *nādhigacchanti*
micchāsaṅkappagocarā"

[They take untruth for truth; they take truth for untruth; such persons can never arrive at the truth, for they hold wrong views.]

Asāre: Lit, essenceless; according to Commentary, right view,i.e., untruth.

Sāre. lit, essence; according to the Commentary, right view, i.e., truth.

Sāraṃ: Truth-According to the Commentary, essence of the *Dhamma.* The essence of the *Dhamma* comprises *Sila, Samādhi, Paññā, Vimutti, Paramattha and Nirvāṇa.*[39]

The term *Paramattha* (Skt. *Paramartha*) means absolute standpoint. Such as in the first sentence of *Abhidhammasatthaṅgaho: "Tattha vuttābhidhammatthā catudhā paramatthato, cittaṃ cetasikaṃ rūpaṃ nibbānamiti sabbathā"* (According to the absolute standpoint, there are four *Dhammas* belonging to the *Abhidhamma* namely, *Citta, Cetasika, Rūpa* and *Nibbāna*).

The opposite term of *Paramattha* is *Sammuti* that means relative or conventional point. For instance, "the table" we see with our eyes is from the relative point. According to the absolute standpoint, the thing named "table"consists of mechanical energy and characteristics. Or we can take another example. We see a gold-ring differing from a gold-necklace (in *sammuti* aspect), but both are made of gold *(paramattha).*

In the same way, when preaching discourses, the Buddha often used the terms man, woman, beings, human-beings *(sammuti).* But in *Abhidhamma,* what the Buddha used are *Khandha, Āyatana, Dhātu-(paramattha).* Or the whole mundane and supramundane things *(sammuti)* are composed in four *Dhammas: Citta, Cetasika, Rūpa* and *Nirvāṇa (paramattha).*

In Buddhist philosophy, the Truth is of two kind : *Sammuti- sacca*(Skt. Samvrit-satya: conventional/empirical/relative or worldly level truth) and *Paramattha-sacca*(Skt. *paramartha-satya*: ultimate/absolute/higher or transcendental truth).

39. Daw Mya tin, Op.Cit., p.5,fn. 1,2,3, verse 11.

9.1 Relative truth.(Sammuti-sacca).

A search for truth is an essential feature of philosophers and religions. Men feel tiny before phenomena and vicissitudes of life. Many metaphysical questions have been subjects for men to ponder as soon as the Buddha's time of more than 2500 years ago, as doubts of *Māluṅkyaputta* put to the Buddha in *Majjhima Nikāya II.*

In verse 70, *Dhamma* refers to the Four Noble Truths *(Catu Ariyasacca).*

> *"Māse māse kusaggena*
> *bāho bhuñjeyya bhojanaṃ*
> *na so **saṅkhātadhammānam***
> *kalaṃ agghati solasiṃ".*

Saṅkhātadhammānaṃ : who have well-weighed the Law, Max Muller and Burlingame. "Who well have taken things into account", Mrs. Rhys Davids. "who have studied the Dhamma noble", Woodward. The commentarial explanation is: "The Ariyas who have realized the Four Noble Truths"[40]

[The prolonged, so-called meritorious fasting of alien ascetics who have not destroyed the passion, is not worth the sixteenth part of a solitary day's fasting of an Ariya who has realized the Four Noble Truths].

The Buddha-the Enlightened One-who has caught the Truth. The first sermon He delivered to the five ascetics was *Catu Ariyasacca.* However the term *"Sacca"* in Pāli (*Satya* in sanskrit, derived from *"sat"*, being), is not an ultimate truth, but the factual truth or actuality, experienced without delusion. Through *Ariyasaca,* the Truth is to be found in the relative conditions of things and events, of cause and its result; to know the truth is to know and see things as they really are *(Yathā-bhūta-ñāṇa-dassana),* which is not a comprehension of

40. Nārada Thera, Dhammapada, notes of verse 70

the ultimate substance of matter, but an understanding of the phenomenal nature of material qualities. So this truth is a relative knowledge. It is itself *Dhamma* which whether a *Tathāgata* arises in this world, or whether no *Tathāgata* has arisen, still it remains a fact that life is suffering *(dukkha)*; this suffering is due to Ignorance *(Avijjā)* and Craving (*Taṇhā*) and the way out of this is the Noble Eightfold Path.

All the Buddha's teachings are the Truth---relative or factual truth. It is the means to achieve the highest goal of life: the ultimate truth, *Nirvāṇa*.

9.2 Ultimate Truth (Paramatthasacca).

It is that which ascetics, monks of any religions ceaselessly tried and are trying for. To Buddhism, that is *Nirvāṇa,* the highest goal of homeless life.

The term *Nirvāṇa* (P.*Nibbāna)* derived from the root Nir+Vā (Nir: to cut, Vā: to blow). It means blown out, gone out , put extinguished. According to Commentaries, it is "Freedom from Desire." *Nirvāṇa* constitutes the highest and ultimate goal of all Buddhist aspirations,i.e. absolute extinction of existence. The word is derived from the root meaning extinguished through lack of fuel, and since rebirth is the result of desire *(taṇhā),* freedom from rebirth is attained by the extinguishment of all such desire. *Nirvāṇa* is therefore, a state attainable in this life by right aspiration, purity of lile, and the elimination of egoism. This is the cessation of existence, union with Ultimate Reality. The Buddha speaks of it as "unborn, unoriginated, uncreated, unformed," contrasting it with the born, originated, created and formed phenomena.

Dhamma in verse 205 is used in this meaning:

'Pavivekarasaṃ pitvā
Rasaṃ upasamassa ca
Niddaro hoti nippāpo
***Dhammapīti** rasaṃ pivaṃ."*

[Having had the taste of solitude and the taste of perfect peace (of Nirvāṇa), one who drinks in the joy of the essence of the *Dhamma* is free from fear and evil].

Mādhyamika school also holds these two kinds of Truth, [while to *Vijñāna-vāda* or *Yogācara* school, there are three degrees of knowledge: *parikalpita* and *Paratantra* correspond to *Sammuti-sacca* and *Parinispanna* to *Paramattha- sacca*], but they are somehow identical with knowledge. The relative level consists of man's reasoning and its products. It causes man to see the universe and its manifold phenomena, and to consider them as real. Due to taking it as real, beings crave for them and try grasping them (Buddhist technical term, beings due to ignorance covering the Buddha-nature)-as a man in dream feels happy and unhappy along with what happening in his dream. Only having waked up, he immediately recognises all those to be unreal visionary. We distinguish ourselves and anothers, subjects and objects, *saṃsāra* and *nirvāṇa*. However *Saṃsāra* and *Nirvāṇa* are two sides of the same hand. Just as pure and impure water in the same cup of water. We can't deny one side of our hand, as well as can't desire pure water while throwing away the cup of impure water. Therefore this relative level is necessary, according to *Nāgarjuna*. Because the absolute level can be understood and realized only by the removal of relative truths. Defilement itself is *Bodhi*. It is here, in this life to be *Nirvāṇa*. We can't find *Nirvāṇa* beyond this visionary world. This is the positive idea of *Mahāyāna*, representative through the image of *Bodhisattvas*, great beings who know all as relatives, being component parts of the same body, courageously enter into the world to undertake beings' trouble, to help people and at the same time to develop their own *Bodhicitta* to attain the highest goal of life, *Nirvāṇa*.

The T'ien-T'ai followed *Nagarjuna* holding *"sūnyata"* to be the central ideal of its philosophy. There is no true state or noumenon besides phenomenon, no difference between *Saṃsāra* and the *Nirvāṇa* or *Sūnyata* (reality). In order to avoid thinking noumenon versus phenomenon, they established the threefold Truth: Truth of Void, Truth of Temporariness and Truth of Mean.

All things are produced by causes and conditions, they do not have any independent reality; they do not possess any self- nature. When these causes and conditions disappear, these things also disappears. Hence they are said to be empty *(sūnya)*. This is called Truth of Void or the truth breaking through subjective illusions. But the emptiness of the *dharmas* does not mean nothingness. It temporarily exists as phenomenon. This is called the Truth of Temporariness or the truth of establishment, since it establishes the *dharmas* temporarily, where they can be reached by the senses. However things neither exist nor non- exist.

Neither "Exist" because it is empty nor "Non exist" because it enjoys existence as phenomenon. This is the Truth of Mean or Middle. This middle doesnot mean something between the two, it is over and above the other two.

These three truths of the Tien Tai school emphasize the idea of totality and mutual identification, the whole and its parts are identical. *"One thought is the three thousand worlds"*---a thing or being is the true state and that the true state is immanent in everything. When this applied to the religious life, it means that phenomenal life is not denied but affirmed absolutely. The everyday life of the layman is part of the life of the Buddha.

The identification of phenomena with the absolute is further illustrated by the Tien-Tai doctrine of the Absolute Mind (to *Yogācara* is *Alayavijñṅṇa*). This absolute mind embraces the universe in its entirety. All things in the world depend on this mind for their existence. This absolute mind originally and for all times contains two natures, one is pure and the other impure. It is the ground of all phenomena, in other word, the *Tathāgatagarbha* (Buddha treasury), Dharma realm. *Nirvāṇa, Sūnya, Paññā, Bodhicitta, Buddhatā, Dharmakāya. Bhūtatathatā, Tathatā*--- the ultimate and unconditioned nature of all things. It is neither one, since it pervades everything, nor multiple, since it remains identical with itself. So, *Dharmakāya* is in everyone. Everybody has the potention to become Buddha.

9.3 The Way to the Ultimate Truth

The way leads to *prajñā* to attain the ultimate truth *(Sūnyata* or *Nirvāṇa)* is not beyond the threefold *Sīla-Samādhi* and *Paññā*.

Keeping precepts in order to prevent and destroy defilements of mind, in other side, to develop the good qualities which is helpful to practise Meditation. Meditation leads to concentrated mind which conditions the appearance of wisdom *(paññā)*. However, we should remember that *paññā* is not produced from *Samādhi*. Just as the pure nature of water is due to keeping the cup of impure water immobile, the dust particles go below and the purity appears. Just as the clarified nature of mirror is not due to cleansing all dust covering it. The nature of clarity of mirror is natural, is characteristic of mirror, however, because of the cover of dust so it seems there is not. Now we cleanse dust, the clarified nature appears. It's also the same case of the image of the moon on the bottom of a river. When being shaked by winds and waves, water filled with dirt, it seems there is no moon there. When there is neither wind nor waves, water stands still and becomes pure, the moon appears. Similar is the case of *Samādhi* and *Paññā*. And once *Paññā* flares up, ignorance disappears. As a lamp brought into the darkened room, the dark disappears at once. We see things clear as they really are. This is the liberation *(vimutti)*. The comprehension of "I am freed" is *Vimutti-nānadassana.*

When we achieve *prajñā*, we reach the state of absolute truth *(paramattha-sacca)* which is beyond thought and conception, unconditioned, indeterminate. This absolute truth cannot be preached in words, but in order to indicate, it is called *Sūnyata* (Reality). "*Sūnyata is the synonym of that which has no cause, that which is beyond thought or conception, that which is not produced, that which is not born, that which is without measure*". *Sūnyatā* itself is *Nirvāṇa.*

It is because *Paññā* is *Buddhatā (Buddha-nature)*, something that is always present in oneself, Ch' an school (Dhyāna school) holds the view that man has ability to apprehend it by intuition directly, completely, and instantly without the need of following steps by steps the procedure of *Sīla-Samādhi-Paññā*. In order to apprehend the Buddha nature, one must calm the mind-Meditation in every moment of life to observe the innermost mind or nature in tranquillity. Reciting the *suttas*, worshipping the Buddha images, or performing the rituals are really of no avail and should be abandoned. Instead, one should allow the mind to operate freely, spontaneously, and naturally.

Anyway, "*there are many paths leading to Roma*" Similarly, there are lots of means in Buddhism leading to the only goal of life: the absolute truth or *Nirvāṇa.*

> "*Sabbadānaṃ dhammadānaṃ jināti*
> *Sabbarasaṃ dhammaraso jināti*
> *Sabbaratiṃ dhammarati jināti*
> *Taṇhakkhayo sabbadukkhaṃ jināti.*"

(Dhp. 354)

[The gift of the *Dhamma* excels all the gifts; the taste of the *Dhamma* excels all tastes; delight in the *Dhamma* excels all delights. The eradication of craving (i.e., attainment of Arahatship) overcomes all ills *(saṃsāra-dukkha)*].

CONCLUSION:

This is an analytical study of the concepts of Dhamma depicted in the *Dhammapada* Sutta. Through each part of the research we can get a rather careful look of the position and worth of the *Dhammapada* in the entire *Buddhavacana*.

We have passed through various concepts as conveyed in the *Sutta*. Besides the popular concept of the Buddha's teachings, i.e. *Tipiṭaka*, this valuable work has revealed that *Dhamma* is also used in the sense of *Cetasikas*, especially volition *(Cetanā)*, the major essence in forming *Kamma* of human-beings. Hence it is said *"Cetanā itself is kamma"*. *Dhamma* is also used in the conception of "Law"-five orders or process which operate, in the physical and mental realms in which the Law of Kamma is the only one. *Dhamma* is also interpreted as Just, Righteous, a good way or pratice *(Dhamma* or *kusalakamma)* and unjust, unfair *(Adhamma* or *Akusala kamma)*. It's also as phenomena in general, composed of all conditioned and unconditioned things including *Nirvāṇa* or it is *Nirvāṇa* itself etc.

People from existences to existences circled in the *Saṃsāra* of rebirths. The Buddha through *Tipiṭaka* in general, and particularly in the *Dhammapada*, has showed the only way *Sīla-Samādhi* and *Paññā*, and because of beings with various levels of mind, so thirty-seven *Bodhipakkhiyas* are divided to suit each of them. However, it is generally stated that either Sīla-Samādhi-Paññā, or the Noble Erghtfold Path or thirty-seven Bodhipakkhiyas, all needed to do is through the practice of Meditation---*Samatha* and *Vipassanā*. It is Meditation--the only path for the purification of beings, for the overcoming of sorrows and griefs, for the going down of sufferings and miseries, for winning the intuitive wisdom, for realising Nine Transcendentals in which *Nirvāṇa* is the highest, a state of cessation of existence, the Ultimate Reality.

Thus, through 423 verses of the *Dhammapada*, 48 verses in which the term *Dhamma* is used to convey nine concepts. The interesting discovery must stimulate scholars about the prosperity of *Dhamma* contained in the whole *Tipiṭaka*. It will certainly be a good and high-appreciated topic for those who thirst for a rather complete knowledge of wider concepts of *Dhamma*, the term with diversified, deep and philosophical aspects in almost ancient Indian religions, specially in Buddhism.

Over two thousand and five hundred years have been passing by! How many vicissitudes of human-being's history are! In spite of all phenomena changing due to the nature-rules of impermanence, each word of Buddha's teachings in *Tipiṭaka* generally, in the *Dhammapada* particularly, still maintain its eternal value. It is quite not surprising when the great commentator *Buddhaghosa* gave a comparison of the teachings of the Buddha with four *Sāgaras,* four great oceans unfathomable in their every respect.

BIBLIOGRAPHY

(1) AMBEDKAR, B.R: *The Buddha and His Dhamma*. Bombay, Siddharth College Publication, 1957.

(2) BAPAT, P.V: *2500 years of Buddhism*. New Delhi, Publication Division, 1964.

(3) BARUA, Beni Madhab and S.Mitra: *Prakrit Dhammapada* (Introduction)

(4) BEAL, Samuel: *Texts from the Buddhist Canon. (Dhammapada)*. London, Triibner and c.o. Ludgate Hill, 1878.

(5) CH'EN, Kenneth K.S: *Buddhism in India*. America, Princetion University Press, 1969.

(6) CHONTHIEN, Ven, Thich: *Phat Hoc Khai Luan*. Giao Hoi Phāt Gia'o Viet Nam, Ban Giao Duc Tāng Ni, 1993.

(7) DASGUPTA, Surendranath: *A History of Indian Philosophy* (vol.IV, Dharma). India, Shri Jainendra Press, 1975.

(8) DAVIDS T.W.Rhys: *The Questions of King Milinda (Book I)*. India,Shri Jainendra Press. 1992.

(9) DAVIDS, T.W. Rhys and WIlliam: *Pāli-English Dictionary*. London, The Pāli-Text Society, 1972.

(10) DAYAL, HAR: *The Bodhisattva Doctrine in Buddhist Sanskrit Literature*. India, Shantilal Jain, at Shri Jainendra Press, 1978.

(11) DHAMMARATANA, Bhikkhu U: *Buddha and Caste System*. Lucknow, Standard Printers, 1969.

(12) GEIGER, Wilhelm: *Pāli Literature and Language*. Trans. by Batakrishna Ghosh. Delhi, Oriental Books Reprint Corporation, 1978.

(13) GELIGER, Willhelm: *The Mahāvaṃsa*. Nice Printing Press, 1993.

(14) KASHYAP, Bhikkhu J: *The Abhidhamma Philosophy (Vol I)*. Delhi, A.K. Distributors, 1982.

(15) LAW, Bimala Churn: *A History of Pāli Literature*. Delhi, Goyal Offset Printers, 1983.

(16) MULLER, F.Max: *The Dhammapada*. India, Shri Jainendra Press, 1992.

(17) MINHCHAU, Most Ven. Thich: *Phāp Cū (Dhammapada)*. Vien Dai Hoc Van Hanh, 1982.

(18) MINHCHAU, Most Ven. Thich: *Thang Phap Tāp yeu Luān (Tāpl)*. Vien Dai Hoc VanHanh, 1971.

(19) NARADA, Thera: *A Manual of Abhidhamma*. Srilanka, The Colombo Apothecaries, 1980.

(20) NĀRADA, Thera: *The Buddha-Dhamma or The Life and Teaching of the Buddha*. New Delhi, Asian Educational Services, 1942.

(21) NĀRADA, Thera : *The Dhammapada*. London, John Merry, 1959.

(22) OLDENBERG, Hermann: *The Dīpavaṃsa*. U.P., Gayatri Offest Press, 1992.

(23) RADHAKRISHNAN, S: *The Dhammapada*. India Jai Ganest Offest Printers, 1992.

(24) ROGERS, R.E. Captain I: *Buddhaghosa's Parables*. New Delhi, Alok. Publications, 1977.

(25) SANTINA,Peter D.: *Fundamentals of Buddhism*. Taiwan, The Corporate Body of the Buddha Educational Foundation, 1984.

(26) SARAO, K.T.S. *The Origin and Nature of Ancient Indian Buddhism*. Delhi, Orient Offest, 1989.

(27) TIN, Daw Mya: *The Dhammapada*. A reprint of Burma Piṭaka Association Publication. Delhi, Photo Offsets Printers, 1990.

(28) WINTERNITZ, Maurice : *History of Indian Literature (Vol.II)*. Delhi, Shantilal Jain at Shri Jainendra Press, 1983,

INDEX

Y